PLAYLIFE

How to Retire before You're Thirty

Dennis Wall

PARTRIDGE
A Penguin Random House Company

To order additional copies of this book, contact
Toll Free 800 101 2657 (Singapore)
Toll Free 1 800 81 7340 (Malaysia)
orders.singapore@partridgepublishing.com

www.partridgepublishing.com/singapore

CONTENTS

PREFACE

This book is written for my children. As a predominantly absentee father, I have not had the privilege to bring up most of you. Although we have spent a lot of time together, I have always lived interstate or overseas. Absentee Dads tend to be "good time" fathers. Visits are more like holidays than real life and you don't really get to impart the values and life lessons that you would like. In a way then, this is an attempt to make up for that.

We have actually spent a lot of time discussing many of the things in this book, but I understand that not everyone is ready for a Dads advice when Dad is ready to give it—just ask my own father! So this is a collection of the things we have talked about over the years, put together as a sort of reference manual.

It's also for my younger kids incase I'm too grumpy an old man to talk through all this with you, when you are old enough to want to know. You may disagree with my thoughts and that's absolutely fine. This is just my take on life—and how to retire before you are 30 (or any age really). If just one piece of advice is helpful to any of you, then putting it writing will have been worthwhile.

Dennis Wall

The first part is general stuff. I will cover ways I have tried to deal with some of my own failings as well as the best way I know to live a noble and fulfilling life. I can't pretend to have got all this right by the way! You kids know as well as anyone that I have messed up a bit along the way but I have conveniently left those bits out of this book! (It's not an autobiography after all). In some instances it's a clear case of do as I say, not what I do. Living with this apparent hypocrisy is part of the battle of being a parent—which you will find out soon enough.

The second part is about the simple secrets of becoming wealthy enough to stop working for someone else by the time you're thirty. If you miss that date by the way, no big deal. The same approach applies at any age (I didn't start on this plan till I was 40 and then retired at 49) but the sooner you start, the easier it is.

Stocks and property will do it—but you have to use them properly and I try to explain just that. If you like money then part two will be the best part of the book. Some of you don't I know, so I've tried to write about money in as interesting a way as possible. Like it or not, money is the key to getting where you want to go, as well the key to providing for yourself and your family in the future. There will be no pensions or other State support for your generation.

Probably it will make most sense if you read "Responsibility" first followed by "Happiness", and then "The Key". I put "The Key" at the end as a summary but it can also serve as an introduction so that you know where I am going with all this. After that you can just wander around the pages that are relevant to you at any particular time. It will be more useful if you only read the bits you want when needed, rather than read it all quickly and then throw it out!

This world is in a bit of a mess at present. We are destroying the environment at a shocking pace. It seems that the only economic model my generation knows, doesn't work anymore and religion is turning more people against each other today than it ever has (which is saying something!) Do what you can to make your own life as good as possible, but always try and do a little bit to improve the world as you go.

Kids, I love you all and admire what you have already achieved in life despite (hopefully not because of) my absence when you were growing up. I hope that this book can help to make your goals even more attainable.

Den (Feb 2014).

PART ONE

GENERAL STUFF

Responsibility

The way to achieve the life you want is to take responsibility for it. The victim mentality is all pervasive in our society. People sue the hardware store because the store didn't warn them that the ladder they purchased could be dangerous if placed in a bath full of water whilst changing a light bulb! Just listen to every whinger on the news who reckons that "the government ought to do something" about everything that's wrong in their lives.

Nobody owes you anything. It is up to you to get on with providing for yourself and future families. If you get pulled up by the police because your tail light is out, is that their fault for being so petty? No it's **your** fault for not fixing it. Is it the company's fault that they don't pay you enough? No it's **yours**—you haven't demonstrated that you are adding value, or you are too lazy to get a new job. The list goes on. The point is to stop blaming everyone else for everything.

Start taking responsibility for your own life from finances to fitness—for every single action. You can choose how you respond to situations. When things look a bit tough or you are losing your cool, take a deep breath and step back from the situation to gain perspective of the bigger picture. Then ask yourself what action you can take right now to improve things. There is always something even if it's shut your mouth for half an hour while everyone else cools down! Take that action immediately and the world will be a little bit better place.

Happiness

Many people the world over are struggling just to survive. Working at jobs they hate (if they have a job) they can barely afford the necessities of food and shelter. In this environment, anger just builds up and up until it explodes spreading violence and hatred all over the place.

People hate other people who have more than they do. They turn to crimes of greed and frustration. The jails are full of people who commit stupid, thoughtless crimes mostly because they have no future anyway, so the consequences of their actions are no big deal. Jail is no deterrent because to many it's not all that different to living "outside".

Many times I notice in the Australian newspapers, the excuse for a violent crime is that the offender was either drunk or under the influence of illegal drugs! Talk about not taking responsibility. What is worse is that this excuse seems to be an acceptable defense to the courts. There is a great example of the lack of individual responsibility being reinforced in a culture through the legal system. Little wonder that the masses take to this excuse with such vigour.

In a developing country with endemic poverty, stealing or begging for a living may truly be an almost inescapable way of life. In developed countries of the free world (like Australia), there is absolutely no excuse for living such a life because there really is an alternative.

If you ask most people in Australia or any other "western" country what they seek most, I suspect that the most common answer would be "happiness". (In most Asian countries by the way, for cultural as well as fundamental reasons, the answer is almost always "money"). The book stores are clogged with titles like "How to Achieve Happiness". The corporate advertising that surrounds us, sets it for us as a target, and then tells us how their products can achieve it! The US constitution includes the pursuit of happiness as an inalienable right alongside life and liberty!

But if happiness is the goal and everyone is striving to achieve it, then why are so few people **actually** happy? Look around. Are your friends, your family, your workmates happy? Are you happy? What would it take to make you happy?

Common answers to this question are: more money, a more fulfilling job, travelling, a more understanding partner, a bigger house/car, a boat, living in a warmer climate, not having to work, more sex and the list goes on. I refer to all these as "fools goals". Distant things that you somehow think when achieved will make you happy. But will they?

I have been through this list in my own life. I have changed jobs, got more money, got divorced, bought bigger houses, bought a boat, moved to a warm climate, retired and had more sex (yes parents **do** have sex!). None of those things made me happy beyond the fleeting glow of any new acquisition.

Now seriously think about this. If what I am saying is true, and the end goal is happiness, then the whole approach to achieving that goal is wrong!

The problem is that happiness is a human emotion and like all emotions, it is transient. No-one can sustain any strong emotion for extended periods of time. You can't be really angry, excited, sad or anything else for long. Extremes of emotion are deviations from the average or the statistical norm—the center path to which all things naturally gravitate.

The trick then, is to make that center path (your normal lifestyle and emotional situation) a path that makes you happy. In other words consider happiness NOT as a goal in itself but as a natural by-product of the life you live. This is a subtle but important definition that can have a profound effect on the way you live and the goals you set.

Happiness is not the end goal but the natural by-product of the life you live every day.

If you accept this definition of happiness, it has huge implications for everything you do. If happiness is a product of the life you live then you really need to know what you want that life to look like. A way to think about this is to consider how you would like to be living when you are say thirty, or (if you can imagine that far out) fifty years old.

How do you want to be generating your income? Where will you be living, what will you be doing most of the time—travelling, diving, sailing, driving, skiing, painting, singing, playing in a band . . . . what?

These are not things that have to be fixed in stone, they can change as experience and income gives you the ability to make different decisions. But you do need to think about your "lifestyle design"—the current trendy word for this process as made popular by Tim Ferris in his book "The Four Hour Work Week" and on his website thefourhourworkweek.com.

If happiness is the result of your lifestyle then it stands to reason that it is not arrived at through the achievement of any one particular or individual goal. If you think that happiness will come when certain goals are achieved, you are going to be sadly disappointed. Every time you achieve a goal, you find that you are no happier and you just head on to the next one thinking that will do it. You are in-fact, just the same unhappy person with another toy. Happiness has nothing to do with the acquisition of assets, toys, wives (husbands) or anything else.

Happiness is the by-product of the life you live.

The most important thing about this statement is that happiness does not need to be deferred until you are living your ultimate lifestyle, in fact the exact opposite! You can be happy most of the time if you employ a key component of many philosophies—living in the present (sometimes referred to as being grounded).

There is no other time than the present. As the statement that has been attributed to many people goes "yesterday is gone and tomorrow never comes". One minute ago is already history, a minute away is still the future. We only live in this current moment. At the risk of sounding a bit of a dribbler, the trick to achieving happiness is to be grounded in the current moment.

If you can't be happy this very minute, it's unlikely that you will be any happier at any time in the future. But how to do this, when you may be worried about your relationship, your income, your debts, your job, and all the other things that fill our "worry time"?

I read a blog by Neil Pasricha called 1000awesomethings. com which has been turned into a book "The Book of Awesome". This book perfectly captures the concept of being happy in the present. It's about appreciating the stuff around you. A couple of my favourites are : "putting on warm underwear straight out of the dryer" or "when a cashier opens up a new lane at the supermarket and you get to go from last in the queue to first"! (For me this is more likely to be when an officer opens a new lane at Immigration, but I get the concept).

It's not unlike the old Sunday school song "Count your Blessings". Look at the good things around you right this minute. Are you sitting with a good friend, is the sun shining, are those warm undies fresh out of the dryer fitting just perfectly? Still struggling to find something? Hell you're breathing aren't you—it could be worse. Old Maurie Laing (my sailing mentor) used to say "every day you wake up is a good day". He was right.

OK that's all a bit brash and shallow but it does work. I know that you are saying that you still have a world of "serious" problems such as those I listed a few paragraphs above and that just smiling about warm undies doesn't make them go away. I hear you. Just refer back to "Responsibility". You can fix all those problems yourself if you shape up to them. All I am saying is that appreciating the moment is the simplest way to achieve that otherwise elusive goal of happiness.

These sections on "Responsibility" and "Happiness" are all the philosophy I have to impart. To be happy, design the life you want, be grounded in the present and take responsibility for everything that happens in your life. You are much closer to achieving all your dreams than you think . . . . much closer.

Fire, Aim

A word of warning about achieving your dreams—time is moving fast, a gazillion times faster than you think. This is good and bad. The good part is you can achieve much more than you think in a very short period of time. When I was 39 I had zero investments (not even my own home) and one failed marriage to show for my life. (On the plus side I also had three of you kids). By the time I was 49, I had fifteen investment properties in two countries, a stock trading business and was living the Lifestyle I had designed a few years earlier.

The bad thing about the speed with which time moves is that if you put things off, you will have achieved absolutely nothing by the time you want to get off the treadmill.

Please, please, please don't waste time

Before you know it you will be fifty and wondering what you did with your life. Whatever it is that you want to achieve, now is the time to do it. One of the calls of the angry birds is "Fire, Aim". That's the order to do things in, otherwise you will spend your life "aiming" but you have no chance of hitting anything unless you "fire". Worse still, by the time you get around to firing, it will be too late.

Procrastination is a common trait, but you can and must learn to overcome it. The easiest way to overcome the P word is to have a clear idea of where you want to be and by when. Try this link http://jamesclear.com/how-to-stop-procrastinating for another way to approach the problem. Then get rid of the time wasters (see below).

What could you be doing right this minute that would help you to achieve your goals? There is always something—do it instead of sitting around doing something else. We are intelligent human beings. We can learn, sadly we often train ourselves to do the wrong things or to do nothing. We **can** teach ourselves to think "what could I be doing now to achieve my goals?" and then to act on that. That's what I mean by "firing". As long as you are firing you will be OK. (And it does help to have a rough idea of the location of the target—see "Decide Who You Want To Be").

Dennis Wall

Time Wasters

You need to decide **who** you want to be, **where** you want to be and by **when**, (see relevant sections below). Everything that does not get you a step closer to those three things is a time waster.

Now I do not include general education, hobbies or family in this category. Family and friends are important in everyone's life (see the section on Family and Friends) and you need to spend time to cultivate these relationships. Just make sure that it's a productive, positive event not just time wasting. For example, a day's sailing, mountaineering, or running with mates I would categorise as positive. A night on the turps with a subsequent two day hangover I would call a time waster.

There are many other timewasters. Chief amongst them is the TV. I know that some of you will insist that TV is educational. I would argue strongly that it is not. Learning from TV is like getting a degree by reading magazines (number two on the timewaster list). The areas covered are always populist, shallow and sensationalised. Anyway be honest with yourself. Once you turn on the box you will watch anything! It's just sucking up your life and turning you into a veggie while you wait to die. Go out and get a life!

Third time waster (after TV and Magazines) is the newspaper. Scan the electronic copy of the front page of the newspaper then forget all the rest of the space filling nonsense and go and do something towards achieving your goals.

There is a "principle" called the Pareto Principle which is more often referred to as the 80:20 rule. Mr. Pareto figured it out in 1906 when he identified that 80% of the land in Italy was owned by 20% of the population. Later he observed that 20% of the pea pods in his garden contained 80% of the peas. This ratio applies to an amazing number of things.

Have a look at your wardrobe. It's a fair bet that 20% of whats in there is worn 80% of the time. In business 20% of your customers give you 80% of your income.

For our purposes, only 20% of what you do is contributing towards your ultimate lifestyle. It probably would make sense to cut out some of that wasted effort that makes up 80% of your time wouldn't it? Most certainly if you are interested in getting to your goal fast.

Who Are You Now?

Part of designing where your life is going to be in the future, is understanding where it is right now. More specifically, you need to understand who you are at the moment and if you want to change that.

How would you describe yourself right now? How would friends or even strangers describe you in one or two words? This is the image that you project, but is this who you want to be in your ultimate new Lifestyle? I believe that it can be helpful when designing your desired Lifestyle, to have a good hard look at who you are (or think you are) today.

I'd always been an introverted, nervous kid. Anxious to do the right thing, be on time and afraid of failure, the advent of the teenage years turned all this around! It was pretty uncool to display these characteristics as a teenager so I adapted a different persona as a coping mechanism.

I adopted a "don't care" attitude (hardly original) and became the noisy, heavy drinking rebel rouser that got me through that terrible period of every young man's life. The problem was that this style of coping accompanied me into adult life. As the senior manager in a multinational company, I was proud to be the last to leave a dinner and then be able to lead my fellow revelers into the seedier parts of most cities in Asia.

This unfortunate style is hard to recognize for what it is— an adopted coping mechanism rather than who I really wanted to be. I actually didn't like the fact that I was expected to be the heaviest drinking, most outrageous person at any event. (I am embarrassed to relate that I am recalled by some as the most drunk Santa at a children's Christmas party, they had ever seen)! Yet without alcohol I felt unable to cope socially. As you can read in the section headed "Alcohol", I figured out how to beat that problem.

Part of being able to beat the booze was to realize that the person I had become was not the real me. That same understanding also helped me to achieve a lot of my other goals. It might help you too.

Everyone adopts a coping mechanism to get through their childhood and teenage years with the least amount of hassle. That persona is a way of behaving that ensures the attention of our parents initially. Then we use it to achieves our other goals and requirements in life. The more this "pretend you" works, the more we use it. We all have insecurities and this role that we develop is the one that also manages to protect us best from the things we fear.

As examples, some adopt the bully strategy deciding that attack is the best form of defense. Others use the victim approach perhaps finding that a sympathetic parent lavished most attention if they played this role. Still others play the fool to avoid the fear of failure by never really trying to achieve anything. A similar result is achieved by being a rebel. Then there are the cynics, who find fault in everything so they themselves cannot be criticised, the perfectionists, the prima donnas, the whingers the work-a-holics and the "Jack the Lads" (a very popular one with the many men who never grow up).

We perfect these roles as we move into adulthood and the workforce and we refine them and re-work them regularly. We do this subconsciously and we end up really believing that this is who we are. We fail to recognize our act for what it is—simply play acting. As mangers, we often find the bully, the perfectionist or the work-a-holic float to the top. When attending courses on better understanding of our own and others personalities, we often view these styles with some pride as evidence of our "type A" successful personality.

If we are to achieve our real goals, our new Lifestyle, we need to have the personal courage to face our demons and undergo some deep introspection to see who we really are. It is that true personality which needs to be satisfied, not the fake one. It is the real you that can relax, laugh, allow others their idiosyncrasies and be genuinely and deeply happy. The pretend you, perhaps the personality with which you achieved your success to date, is still a defense. If you strive to satisfy that personality, to make that person deeply happy, you will fail because that person is just a figment of your imagination!

I don't want to get any more "touchy, feely" than that. Suffice to say that discovering the real you takes courage. It takes some quiet time forgetting who it is that you pretend to be, and listening to that nagging inner voice that is the real you. Sometimes you will need to face fears and insecurities that have been deeply hidden since almost before you can remember. But you **can** remember and you need to let these issues surface, be recognized and dealt with.

Many successful men adopt a façade that professes to enjoy aggressive sports, maybe heavy drinking sessions, a good fight if offended. But the real person may well enjoy something completely different. I bet you know a few of these types of people yourself. I've known many such "type A's" settle down into life in the backwaters on a farm very quickly after leaving work. Seems they weren't really the type they pretended to be after all.

I am not suggesting that you need to start wearing sandals and burning incense! It is simply that without understanding your real personality, you can't be truly happy. Here is a very easy little exercise. Write down the things that you do or participate in regularly. You need a list of at least ten. List sports, leisure and work activities, hobbies and family related things. List anything and everything.

Then clear your mind by doing something else for a few minutes and come back and read through them one at a time. Record with a tick or cross, how the each of them makes you feel, ie does that item make you feel good (tick) or not (cross)? It's a fair bet that the things that make you frown are to do with your pretend persona and the things that make you smile are the real you.

Have a go at being the real you for a while and you might find that you (and others) like it!

Decide Who You *Want* To Be

In the section above, you have worked out who you really are. Now in determining your ultimate Lifestyle you need to decide who you **want** to be. Most people have no idea who or what they want to be when they grow up. Many of us spend our "adult" years waiting to grow up and hoping that someday soon we will learn what it was we wanted to "be"!

I don't think that I am unusual in that I just fell into various jobs. These positions ultimately led me into international management. It's not that I had a plan to do that—it just happened.

Often our career plans are more about getting as much money together as we can, so that we can "retire". Later I'll show you how to make as much money as you want so don't let that colour your decisions.

As far as career and education are concerned, let passion be your guide—not income potential. I read somewhere that 70% of Law students take that path not because they love the thought of practicing the art of argument and acquiring detailed knowledge of how our law works. No, they take that path because they think it will lead to the most possible income! No wonder there are so many dissatisfied lawyers around!

Whatever it is that interests you most, whatever it is that you love, progress that interest to become your career. It doesn't matter if that passion is gardening, animals, diving, finance or travel. If you really have an interest in that path, that's the one that will give you the most satisfaction. Forget about income potential, as mentioned I will explain how to address that later.

If you really want to be a brain surgeon then go for your life and be the best. However, even if you really love brain surgery, you will want to stop doing that one day and spend time doing something else. It's that something else that I am talking about under the heading of "who you want to be".

As mentioned in the previous chapter, this is about designing your lifestyle. Don't worry, nothing is set in stone. At this stage in your life the passion you want to turn into a career might be travel, and you might also want to be a champion skateboarder and that's great. Later you might want to be something else and the plan must be flexible enough to accommodate that.

There is a lot spoken about setting goals and having a vision about the future—all of it over-rated. You don't need to write pages of rubbish and set concrete goals. Just have an idea in the back of your mind how you want to be living at the age of 30. Picture the sort of life you want. Daydream a little, reflect on lifestyles you know or have read about and see how you think yours should look. Maybe you like the way Sir Richard Branson comes across. Perhaps you are more of a Donald Trump or an Angry Anderson. Find a hugely successful person you admire and model yourself on them.

That's all there is to it! Just having that picture in your mind will direct your actions subconsciously toward that Lifestyle. When you look back you will be amazed at how things "just happened" to get you there. Of course they didn't "just happen". When you have that thought of where you want to be in the future firmly in your mind, you automatically make decisions, meet people, ask questions etc that lead you to that place.

I love the natural sciences. I'm fascinated by the world around me and I want to know what makes it work. I absolutely loved the Agricultural Science degree that I did. That's the career I originally embarked upon although fate took me in a different direction very quickly.

The lifestyle I have always aspired towards however was not being a scientist but living on a boat. When I was young, I was mesmerized by the 1960's kids adventure TV show "Adventures of the Seaspray". The widowed father of three was a journalist and the family had one fantastic adventure after another around the tropical waters of the South Pacific on their yacht.

Four years after the start of what is now called the Global Financial Crisis (GFC) I was not a journalist (there are easier ways to fund your lifestyle) but I did co-own a boat with a friend, moored in Thailand. We started having a family holiday on her one week a month. Later I added another week a month with friends or my older kids. Its pretty close to doing exactly as I always dreamed. The Lifestyle design approach really works.

There are some more formal processes you can go through if you wish to use a more traditional way to decide where you want to be. The one below really bought home to me that I was going wrong as a young middle manager and helped me set my life on course.

Write the five things that are most important to you in your life on separate pieces of paper. That is, if you had to select five things and five things only that are important to you and everything else about your life was going to be taken from you by some great power, what would they be?

Then you go through the process of selecting the LEAST important of those five and screwing up that piece of paper. It's a really tough choice because you have already spent some time working out what the MOST important five things in your life are, and now you have to remove one!

Having finally achieved that . . . . do it again. Take the four remaining things that are most important to you and remove the least important. You keep on repeating the process until all you are left with is the single most important thing to you in the world, written on a single piece of paper.

Clearly, modeling the design of your ultimate lifestyle around the single most important thing to you, might be a good idea! Honestly this approach isn't as good for me as just daydreaming about the life I want to live, but it might help you overcome any "writers block" when you're designing your life.

Every time I have done this in a group, most of the group have family or partner, health, financial well-being and happiness on their lists. These outcomes are so incredibly common that I nearly designed this book around those four things. Each of them is indeed covered from different angles in this version of the book. They remain the four key elements to a successful, fulfilling and independent life.

Decide *Where* You Want to be (Three Flags)

I read about the Perpetual Tourist on a website run by Allan R Wallace (http://speculationrules.com/sovereign/pt.php). He is a bit eccentric and the website a bit different, but he introduces the three flag concept originally attributed to Dr W.G. Hill in his book "The Perpetual Tourist". According to Wallace, three flag theory can be summarized as follows:

- Have your citizenship somewhere that does not tax income earned outside the country.
- Have your business in a stable, low or no income tax country.
- Live as a tourist in countries where what you esteem is valued, not outlawed.

The three flags represent the three countries around which you might design your ultimate lifestyle.

Firstly, you need to decide what nationality you want to be—or what passports you will carry. You are a citizen of the world but this flag is home—ultimately if not immediately.

An Australian passport is a handy nationality to have. Australians are not targets of any terrorist organization (for the most part anyway) and the country has a stable political regime, relatively low crime and corruption and is a clean, pleasant place to live. If the world finally goes mad and there is a nuclear war, Australia is just about as safe a place as there could be on the planet. It does not tax foreign earned income if you are a non-tax resident, so it's a good first flag.

Australia however is a socialist country. Socialism is about mediocrity rather than striving for success. Australia is a land of perpetual rights—the right to education, the right to health care, the right to unemployment benefits. As Wallace puts it, that's not freedom, that's dependency. These are not rights, they are the rations of slavery. Another issue with Socialism is that it costs a lot. When you are a geographically huge country with a small population and everyone thinks they are owed a living, the result can only be high taxes.

I advise getting out into the cutthroat world of Asia for a while. You will become a better business person and will build up your wealth much faster than if you stay in Oz. That's what the second flag is about—where you want to earn your income and become a tax resident.

I am not talking about dodgey, zero tax countries known for tax evasion for your second flag. Their days are numbered. I am talking about reputable, well run countries with a more sensible approach to tax than Australia. In the Asian region, Singapore and Hong Kong are the lowest tax, safest and in my opinion the best, for this flag. Their tax levels are less than half of Australia's and they encourage a strong work ethic. You may be surprised to learn that other Asian countries have tax rates pretty close to Australia's. Locals may not pay them but foreigners certainly do.

If you can make it amongst the Chinese business people in Singapore or Hong Kong, you can make it anywhere. Note that being a tax resident does not necessarily mean being a physical resident. It is possible to set up an internet company that earns income in one of these countries without you having to be there. You need a local Director and a locally based accountant (which could be the same person).

If you remain a tax resident of Australia, you will pay tax on income earned anywhere in the world. However, if you set up an internet company in say Singapore, your company will be paying tax in Singapore (17% flat rate for companies at time of writing). The purpose of this money is to fund your third flag (see below) so you will be best to keep the money outside Australia. Set up a credit or debit card facility in Singapore, and use these funds whenever you are in that country or the country you decide is going to be your third flag.

The best way to get to your second flag country is to be sent there by your company. If your company has any prospect at all of sending you abroad—take it! Make it known you are ready to move. No matter what the package, take it. You will be better off in so many ways to get out of Australia for a few years at least.

The third flag is the country where you intend to play. For me that's Thailand/Malaysia. For pleasure boating these countries are unbeatable. You may want to set up another business under your third flag that pays for your expenses whilst there, but that's not essential.

The third flag is a fun flag and not absolutely critical—if you don't want to have fun! It may indeed be many flags if your Lifestyle includes a lot of travel to diverse places. I think it's worth considering a third flag because if your Lifestyle revolves around a particular country, you really want to have things set up so that you can enjoy it to the maximum. That might mean a residence, a boat, a car or other pleasures of home.

Sadly Australia has become absolutely stifling with all the rules it has about what can be done, where. You can't do this, you can't do that. You can't camp here, smoke there, light a fire here, park there, drink anywhere and on the list goes. The Western disease of political correctness means you can't even say what you want to anymore—even in jest! Very little of this applies in Thailand . . . . and I respect that. That's not to say you should behave like a typical visiting Ossie in the country you choose for your third flag. Always remember that you are a guest in that country and treat your hosts and their laws respectfully. I am afraid that if you decide to stay in Australia you will end up asphyxiated—just my opinion.

Alcohol

I don't think that I was an alcoholic, it's just that my entire life revolved around alcohol. My hobbies and sports include social things like sailing and golf, both of which involved substantial use of alcohol. I used alcohol to celebrate, commiserate, relax, sleep, everything. I used to drink every single day and although in later life I learned to delay the first one until (nearly) dinner, once I started I found it very difficult to limit myself to a "sensible" one or two glasses.

I could give up . . . . and often did . . . . usually on a Monday morning with a throbbing headache. We have all said it "I will never drink again" and we mean it. That sort of giving up usually lasts a day or two. Longer periods require much greater willpower mainly because of the length of time we have been using this particular drug and the social and other cues.

Then I found "The Easy way to Control Alcohol" by Allen Carr in a bargain book bin. By the way, this is not the first life changing book that I have found in a bargain book bin. The first was "The Selfish Gene" by Richard Dawkins which I found back in 1984 lying at the very bottom of such a bin having been picked over and rejected by many—judging by the condition of the cover. I rescued it and could not put it down! If you are questioning the religious version of the meaning of life, try The Selfish Gene or any of Dawkins subsequent books.

Carr's book made me realize that many of the things that had messed up in my life were actually as a result of alcohol. Whilst not the direct cause of my failed marriages, booze definitely did nothing to help resolve the inevitable communication problems. The extra 5kg (alright 10kg!) I had been carrying around were a direct result of alcohol consumption. Stupid behavior in bars late at night—well that's obvious. The list goes on.

I am a bit of a conspiracy theorist. It struck me that the whole concept of drinking has to be the single most successful marketing con trick ever! Kids watch their parents having a drink or rabbiting on about a glass of red and naturally want to emulate them. Young kids enjoy nothing more than getting another beer out of the fridge for Dad and his mates! What a shocking lesson to teach them. Booze becomes the thing you want to have most, made more attractive by the fact that you're not allowed to have one!

According to Carr, 90% of the population drinks. Well, in my circle of friends and acquaintances it was 100%. After the initiation of children into the drinking culture, comes the ridiculous peer group pressure to drink more volume and more often—from absolutely everyone you know. "Come on mate, you're very slow" and all the other similar statements, serve to further the marketing for the big alcohol companies. Then there is the absolute baloney around the "appreciation" of wine. I was a leader in this BS amongst my peers, having amassed an impressive, professionally stored cellar of old Australian reds which I had shipped to Singapore on a regular basis as they "matured".

I suddenly realized that I was both the unwitting victim **and** perpetrator of a huge marketing con. I find nothing more offensive than that, so immediately decided that I would give up. It was amazingly simple and problem free. I have tried to have a couple on several occasions just to be sociable, but frankly I don't enjoy it. I did the calculations and realized what a crazy sum of money I had tied up in booze. I gave most of it away and sold the rest.

For the first few weeks of abstinence I was a bit disappointed that I didn't feel better or different. I guess I expected a dramatic improvement but instead that improvement occurred gradually over a longer period. After a couple of months I had never felt better. I was waking up feeling fit and ready to go. I was more patient with everyone around me and in general I became a more balanced person. Now the feeling is one of elation at the freedom I have. I had no idea how much of a shackle around my neck drinking had become.

Some things have changed of course. Sadly I realized that the sum total of my relationship with some people was getting pissed. Needless to say, some of those relationships have been a bit curtailed, but others actually blossomed into something beyond "drinking buddies".

I find that I leave social functions earlier than I used to—which is not hard since I used to be the last person being kicked out, often at sunrise. Getting up after a night out feeling well rested and without a hangover is a feeling without parallel. I think giving up has made me a nicer person, definitely less aggressive and grumpy. And that all adds up to being a better father which is my aim.

I am not evangelical about this in any way. I am very happy for others to drink as much as they like and I always keep plenty of old reds in the wine fridge for those that enjoy them. It's just that I have no intention of getting back into that habit again—ever.

According to Carr, every drinker is somewhere along the continuum from "occasional drinker" to the abject "homeless alcoholic" we all associate with the term. I decided I was far enough along that continuum and that I had better get off!

I had a stack of ploys I used to use when I was giving up booze regularly. I no longer use them because the thought of being a pawn in the marketing game of a few multinationals was all it took for me. You might find them of some help if you try to give up or at least they might give you a laugh.

- Sign up for "Dry July" at dryjuly.com. This is a good idea anyway because you can directly benefit the lives of adults living with cancer across Australia. But it won't help you give up the grog permanently.
- The fitness approach: Two pints of regular beer will take you half an hour of reasonably fast running to burn off. Have a six pint night, and you need to run for an hour and a half just to get that excess energy out of your system. That's **excess** not your regular weight loss. Thought of as minutes of running, a drink seems much less attractive. Trouble is, after a couple you don't care about tomorrow and then with a hangover you are less likely to train anyway. Before you know it, you have lost the mental impetus to keep fit. This approach doesn't work.

- One water, one alcohol: A simple sounding approach that is a lot harder in practice. Even if you don't end up drinking much less, at least you will be less dehydrated next day (meaning hopefully you will have a less severe hangover). Like most of the others, this doesn't work after you've had a few.

- One day at a time: This is a common approach to many addictions; the one employed by AA and thus obviously works. The idea is that forever seems too long so you try and give up drinking just for today. Do the same thing the next day. You can mark off the days on a calendar if that helps. Pretty soon you have strung a few days together. The weakness with this system is that I feel like celebrating if I make a week and celebrating means . . . a drink!

- Doctors' orders: This helps if you feel like you need an excuse (which all Australians do) **not** to drink. It's the one time that your mates will be supportive and it makes you look an idiot if you've told everyone you can't drink because of doctors' orders and then you do drink! Trouble is that at one stage I actually **was** under doctors' orders to give it away and somehow felt like a hero when I ignored that advice.

- Change your habits: The idea here is that there are social cues that make you want a drink. Change those and you feel less like having one. Don't go to the places you normally go, don't socialize with the friends that make you drink, etc. This might work for some people but if you feel like a drink even on your own, this won't be much help.

- Man Boobs: Beer in particular increases your female hormone production and reduces testosterone production (although you would never guess this late at night in most Australian pubs). That's why you get man boobs and a good visual cue that it's time to cut back or stop. Under thirty's are too young to have this problem but keep drinking and they will turn up! Man boobs don't look better with age or a suntan. The problem with this strategy is the well-known ability of men to think they look great no matter how bad they really look! "I could get back into shape in a couple of weeks if I tried". Sure. Fear of man boobs won't stop you drinking.

- Just say "No". There are plenty of times when you are offered a drink that you can simply refuse. Set little rules for yourself that you refuse to break—like nothing before 5pm, or dinner (this has worked for a while for me) or during the week. In the end, this will fail because it's based on willpower and you know how good that is!

Have a good hard look at the benefits versus the cost of drinking. You will find as I did that there are ZERO benefits and plenty of costs. The costs include your personality, physical damage to yourself, others and property, your bank account (drinking is expensive) your career, your family and your goals.

Think about the stupid things you or your friends do when drunk. People end up in jail despite the fact that the courts seem to accept as a reasonable defense for all sorts of antisocial behavior, that the perpetrator was drunk. We have all been in fights, car accidents and other ridiculous situations all because we were tanked—in other words not capable of making sensible decisions. If that's not enough to make you give up drinking you are not yet ready to make a success of your life.

Banks

Banks are much maligned. Everyone seems to enjoy bashing the banks. And why not, we all have to use them but we have no idea what they do. We do know that they are charging us too much, making too much money, not helping the poor and the elderly and on it goes.

Banks are businesses. They exist to make money, like every other business. They are not an extension of the Australian social security system. They do not owe anyone anything except their shareholders for whom they have a responsibility to make a profit.

When someone is declined a loan, is it the banks fault? Of course not—it's the person who failed to save enough, earn enough or is trying to borrow too much. And here we are again taking responsibility for ourselves! It's a great idea to borrow money as addressed later. It's a great idea to have access to good credit facilities. It's also a good idea to live within your means, and make so much money that you don't have to beg banks or anyone else for money.

Funny enough, when you don't need the money you'll find the banks come running to you!

Credit Cards

Recently on the boat, I asked two of my kids if credit cards were good or bad. The immediate response was "Bad" which is very understandable if you have been burnt with credit card debt in the past. But actually credit cards are the best (and maybe the only) source of free money that exists in the world. As a result, I am a great fan of credit cards—if you can use them sensibly.

Using a credit card sensibly is very, very simple—pay it off in full every month. A credit card enables you delay payment for up to 2 months (on those items you purchase straight after the last bill) because you get a bill at the end of the month and then you get a month to pay that.

As well, most cards these days offer loyalty points which I think are junk except that you can convert them to frequent flyer miles! This means that the more you use the card, the more free travel you can undertake. Use it for buying groceries, fuel, paying for phone bills, electricity, everything you can. But make sure that you set up an automatic payment system from an account that will have enough money in it, to pay every cent off when it's due.

If you start paying the minimum required, you are about to be murdered with interest rates that you cannot imagine. That's when credit cards become "Bad" and when they go from providing free money to being just about the most expensive money on the planet. So do not even consider using this facility. Pay all amounts due every single month and take full advantage of this amazing free credit facility.

Also if you use the card enough (usually around $20,000 per year) you can phone the company when they charge your annual fee and they will take that cost off. What a great system—when used properly!

Getting Fit

I read somewhere that the first person that will live to one hundred and thirty years old has already been born. Since I'm already in my fifties (ok *mid*-fifties) that person is probably not me—but I find it vaguely encouraging that it's possible! My parents are in very reasonable condition in their mid—eighties, so barring accidents I am aiming for about one hundred and ten. If you are under thirty now, you should be able to make the one hundred and thirty mark.

However, not only do we want to live to these sorts of ages, we want to be fit and active then—venerable not vegetable. This section is about what I have gleaned to make that outcome more likely.

Just about everything in you new Lifestyle requires you to be fit. To be a good partner, parent and global citizen, you need to be fit. It's just not possible to jump out of bed full of enthusiasm to start the day if you're 20 kg overweight and slightly hung-over!

I have been very fit and I've been very unfit. I can tell you that being fit is by far the better feeling. It's well worth getting unbelievably fit as a youth and staying that way. You will cruise through life knowing there is always that bit more in the tank than everyone around you. It means that you can always find the energy to go kick a ball, swim a few laps or go for a jog no matter how tough your day has been.

I spend a lot of time on my boat and I can't always exercise when I'm away but I don't fret about it. I do work out every single day when I am at home. Days off are not needed with my routine because you give each muscle group plenty of recovery time. Besides which, days off break your routine and make it more likely that you may not start again!

If you want to put on weight (muscle) then the program will be a little bit different to if you want to lose it (fat that is). However it's not complicated. In all cases eat well (more vegies and quality protein—less processed carbs, salt and fat) and exercise heaps. Don't smoke, don't drink (see relevant chapters) and look forward to a long and happy life!

Weight gain or loss is treated as though it's difficult or complex—it's not. Actually it's about the simplest thing there is because it's all about a very basic little equation—the energy equation:

Energy in = energy out. The difference is fat.

There is a whole lot of nonsense written about the type of energy you consume, energy burning foods and other stuff. This is all just garbage used to try and sell fitness or mens/womens magazines. (And while we are at it, there is no food that contains less energy than it takes to metabolise it—including celery).

If you eat more than you burn through exercise and general living, you will get fat. If you eat less, you will lose weight. Nothing is simpler than that. An entire industry is based on making you believe that the game of health and fitness is complex and difficult. Don't get sucked in, just follow the energy equation.

If you want to *gain* weight, eat more of everything especially protein. Use the same exercises as for weight losers, but do low repetitions. Do no more than 30 minutes of aerobic exercise a day (running, swimming, cycling, dance, boxing, etc). No aerobic exercise is needed if you live an active lifestyle. Watch those muscles grow!

If you want to *lose* weight, eat less of everything especially carbohydrates. Instead of heavy weights and low reps (which is for muscle gainers) use light weights and high reps. In addition to your regular active lifestyle, add as much aerobic exercise as time allows—about an hour; more just makes the results come faster. Watch the kilos fall off.

Having said that, people wanting to lose weight will often do as well by following the muscle building plan of low reps heavy weights. That's because this will build more muscle. Muscle weighs more than fat but it also burns more energy. Just do some exercise.

If you are keen to measure things then count calories and chart your progress use an app like MyFitnessPal or one of the many other free apps available. Lots of people recommend measuring yourself before you start an exercise program so that you can detail the benefits. I can't be bothered with that—you will see the benefits soon enough. Do weigh yourself as often as you like (every day is good if you want). Just use the same scales at the same time of day. First thing in the morning before food or drink is the best. If you're moving in the right direction weight wise, great. If not, eat a bit more or less, or do a bit more or less exercise. No need for overcorrection, just keep an eye on things.

An article in the New England Journal of Medicine (13/11/2008) reported on a European study of 359,000 people with an average age of 51.9. That's a lot of people and enough to be pretty sure the results are representative of the broader population. They found that excess fat stored around the middle was a major health risk even when people were not considered over weight by other standards.

A thick waist almost doubles the risk of premature death! Now that is exactly what we are trying to avoid. Every 5 cm increase in waist size increased the risk of death by 17% in men and 13% in women. The solution suggested by the studies authors? Increase the amount of exercise performed every day, avoid excessive alcohol and improve diet. Surprise!

A more recent article published in the Sydney Morning Herald on 15th May 2013 reported on another British study by Dr Margaret Ashwell, presented at the European Congress on Obesity. Her study over twenty years determined that keeping your waist circumference to less than half of your height improves your life expectancy by 17 years over those who don't. This simple measure applies to men, women or children and can be in either inches or centimeters.

For a 185 cm person this means a waist measurement of 92.5cm or less. Nice and simple and a good one to keep an eye on.

I am not a gym junkie. I don't mind the gym but I don't long to be there. The gym itself is not my lifestyle choice but everyone is different. Lots of people need the social stimulus or the competition of having other people around to motivate them. If that's you—great! Join a big city gym with lots of other sweaty bodies and knock yourself out.

For me, exercise is about doing the least possible for the maximum result. Unless your new Lifestyle revolves around spending tons of time at the gym then I suggest you take the same approach.

The "Twenty plus Five" Plan

This section is a result of my training (I was one of the first graduates of the Tasmanian Fitness Trainers Course), a lot of reading and years of practical experience. There are millions of exercise programs, and they all work—if you stick at them. My approach is to get maximum results for minimum effort. The theory being that the less time you have to spend getting fit, the less likely you are to get sick of it!

I call my routine "twenty plus five" because it consists of twenty minutes in the gym—no more—every day and five kilometers of aerobic exercise each day. The twenty is twenty—if you are doing more you're wasting your time and the gym is a lifestyle for you not a place to get fit. The five is five—if you run it, this might take 30 minutes. Walk and it will take an hour. Crawl and it will take two hours or more. It doesn't matter how you do it, just do five kilometers at the fastest speed you can—one that makes you sweat.

If running is not your thing or your knees are no good, substitute the "five" for 45 minutes of any aerobic exercise—swimming, cycling, crosstrainer etc. You are aiming to burn something like 500 calories.

The gym component is equally straightforward. In case you are not up with gym jargon, a repetition or rep is the number of times you lift a weight. A set is a group of reps. So you might lift a weight 10 times (or 10 reps) and that makes up one set. Two sets means lifting that weight another 10 times.

Dennis Wall

The general idea is to exercise every body part every four days. If you want to gain muscle then its heavy weights, low repetitions. You should lift weights that you can only lift a maximum of seven times. As you get stronger and can lift the weight eight or nine times, increase the weight so you can only lift it seven times again. Rest a minute between exercises. Spend only twenty minutes on weights, then stretch thoroughly and leave.

You can do the five kilometers any time. I don't like treadmills and it suits my routine to go to the gym in the mid-afternoon—which I do because there is rarely anyone else there. Then I go for a run late in the evening before the stock market opens at 9:30 or 10:30pm my time (depending on US daylight savings). If its better for you to get sweaty once, then do the "five" immediately before or after the "twenty". Whatever suits you is fine.

Note you only need to do one or two sets per exercise at most. There is plenty of research to show that doing three and four sets has zero additional impact on muscle gain compared to just one or two. Have a look at Tom Ferris book "The Four Hour Body" where he recommends one set only. However, you must do your seven repetitions to failure. Failure means you cannot lift a single gram more! Failure does not mean that you **think** you've done enough. It means if you put every single fibre of your body into it, you just cannot complete the eighth lift.

Personal trainers always ask "what is your goal" gain muscle or lose weight, as if the two are mutually exclusive. They are not mutually exclusive and the "twenty plus five" plan will see you lose weight **and** put on muscle. If you really do want to lose weight, remember the energy equation—eat less! You don't need a personal trainer to tell you what to do. Just do it.

In the Gym, match every exercise with one for the opposite muscle group and then "superset" them. For example, if you want to do say three chest exercises, then match them with three back exercises. Working on biceps today? Pair each exercise with one for triceps. Super setting means to perform one exercise, then with minimal rest, go do one for the opposite muscle group. An example might be bench press then lat pull downs. You get more done in less time with supersets because you are resting one muscle group while exercising another without actually taking the time to rest and do nothing!

The actual exercises you use really don't matter. You can find great workouts at menshealth.com or any of the magazines around. I have found that about 6 exercises, (two sets of seven reps each) fills twenty minutes. Just be sure to cover all muscle groups—that is exercises for back, chest, arms, shoulders, legs and abs. And now I've mentioned them, don't treat your abdominals any differently to any other muscle group. If you work on them every day they will just get fatigued and you'll get sick of it! Once in a four day cycle like everything else is enough.

If you pair them as suggested, you may end up doing chest and back on Mondays, biceps and triceps on

Tuesdays, Shoulders on Wednesdays and Legs and Abs on Thursdays. Then just keep the routine going. You don't need a rest day because it will be four days since the same body part was exercised last.

The beauty of such a short workout every day is that it just becomes a simple routine—like cleaning your teeth! You don't have to put it off because it takes too much time. You can change the exercises if you like—or not. Just make twenty minutes in the gym a daily routine, and don't forget the five kilometers.

Finally, it doesn't matter if you are male or female—do twenty minutes of weights a day plus five kilometers. Girls won't get any bigger muscles than nature allows so don't worry about that. Eating well and exercising results in perfect and natural hormone balance. It's this balance that stops the girls from getting too muscular and the boys from growing man boobs.

Here is the routine. As mentioned you only need to do two sets of each with a heavy enough weight that you can only do seven repetitions.

Day 1: I start with shoulders because they are my weakest and the muscle group that I am most likely to avoid if for some reason I have to skip a days exercise. I do military press, shrugs (forward and backward), bend over lateral raises, medial lateral raises and anterior lateral raises. I also do seated Arnie curls to make up six exercises. Then I pair them and do them as supersets. You can mix and match the pairings, do them in two groups of three or do the six in a circuit.

Day 2: Chest and back. I always look forward to this one. Incline, regular and decline bench press (or dumbbell fly alternatives) for chest. Pair these with front lat pull downs, rear lat pull downs and rows. As before, any alternatives are fine. There are probably more variations on these exercises than any other. Just ensure that you select a weight that only allows you to do seven repetitions to failure. Because these are big muscle groups, you will be able to increase the weights quite quickly—that's why I like day two!

Day 3: Arms—another favourite, the T-shirt muscles. Pick three biceps exercises and pair them with three triceps. Dumbbell curls might be one, preacher curls and hammer curls the other two exercises for biceps. These can be paired with overhead triceps extensions, front extensions (using a close grip on the lat pulldown bar) and say tricep kickbacks.

Day 4: Legs and Abs. My least favorite but it's the end of the routine and I know the fun stuff will start again the next day. Because of the number of different leg muscles, this is the only day that I do four exercise pairs. Four legs paired with four abs is what you need. I do squats or lunges, quad machine and hamstring raises then calf raises. As superset paired exercises I do planks, regular crunches, bicycle crunches and lower back hyper extensions (weighted). I am not a fan of this day because if you work out hard, you ache more from these exercises than any others! Plus its hard to see the improvement. Anyway—they have to be done so best to just do them. It gives all your other muscles a rest day as well.

And that's it. As already stated, any variations are acceptable and there are plenty of other routines that will do the same job. The trick is to make it short and intense, keep the boredom level down and keep the routine going. If you are starting from scratch, the results will be obvious within the first two weeks! If you can keep going for a month you will start to feel superhuman. If you can keep it going for longer than a month (ie forever) you **will** be superhuman!

If you live in a place where a full body massage is available for a reasonable price, you might want to spoil yourself with one or two in the first couple of weeks of this routine. You get mighty sore with this sort of workout and a really stiff neck is enough to stop you going to the gym—which is what we are trying to avoid.

If a brilliant country like Thailand is one of your flags, have a massage at least once a day! An hours Thai massage might cost $6 and for an extra couple of dollars you can have a manicure and pedicure as well. I love the third flag.

Looking (and Acting) the Part

When you get to thirty and you're living the Lifestyle you have designed, you will no longer be going to the office. This is not an excuse to spend all day in your PJ's, not shaving or showering. This is for the old fashioned, old age retiree—not the modern young person who is living their lifestyle by design.

You want to look like the young, fit, healthy and independently wealthy person that you are. Here are a few pointers to make sure that you always look and act the part:

1) Decide how someone with your lifestyle looks best and dress that way every day. This can be an independent look or you can find fashionable icons on the net if you need inspiration. Are you a Richard Branson (open neck white shirt, jacket and jeans) a Steve Jobs/Rupert Murdoch (black turtle necks) or a Kate Perry (cannot describe). I'm a boater. I wear shorts and polo shirts with deck shoes. It reminds me every day who I am and how hard I worked to get here.

2) Don't do stuff you don't want to. It makes you look sour! There will be obligations (like dinner at the in-laws on Sundays) that just have to be done but in the day-to-day sense, you are in control of your life. You will be a happier, healthier person if you spend most time doing what you like doing not what someone else thinks you should do, and you'll look brighter.

3) Don't spend time in a bad relationship. You will look and feel bad, your partner will look and feel bad and life is too short. See the "Life Partners" section. Fix it or leave.

4) Don't forget your friends. For sure they will have ridiculed your plan earlier (because you wouldn't go out drinking with them). Now that you are independently wealthy, they will be saying stuff like how "lucky" you are that you can retire before 30. They may not be financially well

educated but you should still have a variety of friends. It's good for you and no matter who they are, you can learn something from everyone. If they are open minded, you never know, they might end up learning something too!

5) Realise how much your Mum has done for you and make a point of letting her know how much you appreciate it every now and then.

6) Use that famous Pereto Principle (you don't need 80% of what you have) and clear out your life—often.

You may not realize it but if you are living your designed Lifestyle, you are a role model for everyone that has not achieved the same results. If you have done all this and retired before thirty, you are a huge success—behave like it at all times. These days, someone is always watching!

Hats

I grew up in Australia making the most of waterpsorts, mainly surfing and sailing. I never used sunscreen (I'm not even sure it was invented back then) and never wore a hat. Today, some thirty years later, I am having skin grafts and other equally unsightly and unpleasant treatments to remove the basal cell carcinomas that resulted from the UV exposure.

You can avoid all this easily if you are a bit smarter than I was—especially while you are young. Wear Sunglasses. Wear a hat. Wear sunscreen. Wear a shirt in the sun. Slip, slop, slap. Skin cancer is not a pretty thing.

Smoking

Does anyone need convincing that smoking is a very stupid thing to do? Yes . . . anyone who has ever smoked and then has a couple of drinks! You know full well that sucking smoke into your lungs is probably the dumbest thing you could ever do. You are making huge tobacco companies and their shareholders (and the government via taxes) incredibly wealthy whilst you increase your chances of a premature and painful death.

This just doesn't make sense to anyone with an ounce of intelligence, but then along comes a beer or two. That's why giving up both drinking and smoking go hand in hand. After the second beer, intelligent rational thought processes go out the window! Suddenly a smoke seems like not that bad an idea. All the usual excuses present themselves—just one won't hurt, I haven't had one for ages anyway, I'm healthy, everyone else is having one, etc. etc.

This is really not funny—if you smoke you are inviting death and disease into your life. My first wife's Grandfather was a chain smoker who had smoked since he was 12. He told me when he was sixty-ish that he loved smoking and if it meant he died a few years earlier then he was OK with that. The problem was that instead of dying early, ten years later he started losing his legs to smoking related gangrene. First one foot, then the other then the first leg was amputated above the knee! This once fit, active man was reduced to a wheelchair for the last ten years of his life until the cigarettes (which he continued to smoke) finally did kill him.

Don't mess with this. You have more to live for than a huge multinational tobacco companies profits. Just quit smoking and if that means not drinking, do that too.

Apparently half of all smokers are chemically addicted. If you think that's you then you need to buy the patches or gum. Once you are using them, you are like the rest of us, just trying to break a physical habit so the following applies to everyone.

To break a habit, stop doing the things that give you the cues. Maybe its going to the bar after work? Stop it. Drinking? Give up. Getting out of bed? Skip the smoke and go for a run. Identify the cues and break the pattern, change things.

Then you might find some of the things below helpful:

1) Start carrying around a bottle of water with you. Drink it instead of smoking. Buy a fancy sports bottle if you like.
2) Exercise. See the relevant section. Aerobic exercise is especially important. It makes you aware of your dwindling lung capacity and helps you beat the habit.
3) Change your friends. Smokers associate with smokers. If you really want to quit, skip their company for two months. Sure they will ridicule you for a while. Let them, that's their choice. True friends will support you—maybe even join you.
4) Stop drinking. See that section.

5) Have a huge night to celebrate the fact you are going to give up and smoke as much as you can. I managed four packets—it was pretty easy to stop the next day.

6) Have your teeth professionally cleaned immediately after the big night and don't smoke after that. You are less inclined to want to mess up a nice clean mouth with smoke.

7) Give up day at a time—the AA approach. Don't give up "forever" straight off. Just give up for today. Then tomorrow do the same thing. Days turn into weeks pretty fast and so on.

Giving up smoking is easier than drinking because it's an innately ridiculous thing to do in the first place. Just think about what you are doing. Sucking smoke into your lungs from a lighted stick of rolled up leaves was a dumb idea even before they took all the goodies out of the tobacco. At least originally you used to get a nicotine high. Now you don't even get that!

Yes I was a "social smoker". And like drinking, I am not fanatical about being a non-smoker. For example I will have a cigar when a friend's baby is born. Even though I don't enjoy it, I know I could easily smoke an entire packet of cigarettes if I had enough to drink and was in the wrong company! That's one of the reasons that I don't drink. Having designed my new Lifestyle I really want to live long enough to enjoy it.

Eating

As mentioned in the exercise section, gaining or losing weight is about exercise and the energy equation. To repeat:

Energy in = energy out. The difference is fat (gain or loss).

When you are young, your metabolism is faster and you can get away with a bad diet, drinking and not doing much exercise whilst remaining reasonably trim. This magical time stops by the time you are around thirty.

From then on you have to work at keeping fit. The food side is easy and you already know it for sure. Just don't eat the bad stuff: fats, sugars (simple carbohydrates), salt. Do eat more protein and more vegies (especially green vegies). Eat just enough to feel full, and stop then. If you don't need desert, don't have one. (You know you don't need desert).

There are lots of fad diets out there. They don't work and are impossible to stick to. Just eat sensibly, stop eating when you've had enough and don't drink your calories (soft drinks and alcohol).

Snack on nuts, cold chicken, cheese, fruit etc. Drink water. You can eat regular meals or graze, it really doesn't matter. Just keep the energy equation in mind and you will be fitter than most.

If you want to be super muscular and impress everyone at the beach, then you'll need a much more specific diet which is beyond me to provide. I found ABS DIET POWER from Mens Health an absolute winner though if you need something more than just sensible eating. It's a bit like the Atkins diet in that you get to eat as much as you like of a stack of great things. Go to www.menshealth.com for the full story.

Religion

Religion is based on a concept called Faith. Faith can be defined as the irrational belief in the existence of something (or someone) invisible, supernatural, generally unsubstantiable.

If such a belief is held about Father Christmas or the Tooth Fairy, you are probably under six years old and everyone else is enjoying your childish gullibility. If the belief is about Martians, flying saucers or the Loch Ness Monster then the proponents are either locked away or just treated like fruitcakes. If the irrational belief is religious in nature (about a "God") however, we are all forced to treat it as something that should be respected!

Travel is mind expanding and one of the things you see when travelling is the plethora of different religions around the world. All preach that theirs is the only true way to salvation and their God(s) alone should be worshiped. Naturally when you think about this you realize that they can't all be right—infact by logical extension, they must all be wrong! The only reason that most people belong to any particular religion is an accident of birth. Where you were born always affects the folk stories you are told.

Religious beliefs should be treated like everything else in life: do not blindly accept anything some-one else tells you is truth.

Question everything that is presented as fact. Keep questioning until you are satisfied with the answer. If you cannot get satisfactory answers and you still thirst for knowledge about life's great questions, read "The Selfish Gene" by Richard Dawkins or any other of his many books.

The biggest problem I have with religion is that whilst tolerance is a widely preached theme, it is rarely genuinely practiced. Look around the worlds conflict zones and you will find many driven entirely by opposing religious views.

Having a strong code of ethics does not require religious belief. Stick to your ethics, educate yourself, try to educate others and don't believe there are fairies at the bottom of the garden just because someone else does.

Family and Friends

No one is an island. You need to have family and friends around you to grow as a person, to share experiences with and to love. No matter who you are or how strong an individual you are, happiness will elude you without good friends and loving family around.

Be a good friend. Dogs are the best friends so to be a good friend, behave like a dog. Dogs love you without expecting anything at all in return, they love you even if you don't have food. They don't say much but they are always there.

Think about what you want from your friends. Someone who doesn't judge, someone who listens, shares time, helps out, offers advice only when asked, is dependable and so on. Be that person to your friends. Friends are not people that can get you somewhere, do something for you or are names you collect on Facebook. They are what keep you grounded, sane and happy. Collect as many as you can but also be one to as many people as you can.

They say you can choose your friends but you can't choose your Family. That's true, but if you read Dawkins "the Selfish Gene" you will understand that family is part of your genetic survival. That's the biological reason why you should care for your family. In practice, your siblings and even your parents and grandparents can number among your closest friends.

When you become a parent, you appreciate even more why your own parents care for you so much, forgive most of your shortcomings and defend you at all times against the rest of the world!

Numerous studies have found that friendship is an important part of living longer and being happier. If you have moved interstate or overseas for a while, one of the difficulties of returning is that the friends you left behind all seem to still be doing the same things as when you left! That's kind of nice but also kind of depressing. Don't bang on about all the wonderful things you've been doing. Listen to whatever has been happening in their lives. That's what friends do.

Strive for your goals, work hard, get fit, be the best you can be at all things, but don't forget to keep in touch with your family and friends. Your newly designed Lifestyle will probably include a lot of different activities and this is where new friendships are formed. Make the most of being exposed to a wide range of people to whom you have nothing to sell! Its fantastic to appreciate people for who they are rather than what they can do for you. The most interesting people listen actively (ask lots of relevant questions) and rarely talk about themselves. Lets be interesting!

I have found that my life partners often don't like my friends! That's absolutely fine, they are **my** friends. I have close friends that I went to pre-school with. I have really good friends that I have only known for a year or so. Some of my friends are professionals, some are unemployed (and unemployable). What people do, or how much they earn does not make any difference when it comes to friends. Don't be judgmental and be a good friend.

Life Partners

I have been married three times. Each time started out fantastically and ended up pretty much the same. Every time my partners seemed to change—for the worse. Those fun loving, happy girls became boring stay at homes! How could this have happened to me three times?

Closer analysis of my relationships revealed one common factor . . . . me! Was it possible that *I* was the reason for these failed relationships? Could it be that there was something about my own behavior that was causing the change in the behavior of my spouses? Ofcourse you blockhead!

If you live with anyone long enough, they will get on your nerves—and you theirs. This applies to friends, family, lovers, spouses in fact every human being (but interestingly not to dogs)! After five or even ten years you are faced with a decision—make a huge swath of compromises and excuses and stay in a relationship that is only going to get worse, or quit.

Put this way the answer seems obvious but actually it isn't that clear. Either alternative has its downside. For the quit option, which so often seems the best, the biggest downside is "how many times can you do this". Much depends on your personality, your appetite for risk and your finances. For sure however, if the compromise option requires you to change your personality or style or your partner to change theirs, the sooner you get out the better.

You may indeed want to make changes to your style or fix some flaws, but to change the essence of who you are is not going to happen and certainly should not happen, to please someone else. I spent decades trying to change my partners—as they did with me. What a wasted life! When the romance (Dad talk for sex) died down, as it inevitably does, what was left? Was I going to be stuck with an unloving spouse forever? Oh poor me.

I wish I had known all about taking responsibility for my own life back when my first marriage failed. No-one owes you a dream relationship that will last forever. Actually there is no such thing. There is no perfect relationship. Just cast a glance at the news to see the litany of failed marriages among the rich and famous. Apparently neither good looks, wealth, fame nor success, are a guarantee of a long and happy relationship.

My advice is that if you have settled down with a reasonably sane person, made some commitments, maybe had children, then for goodness sake suck it up and try and make it work! Your life may not be perfect but it probably is pretty good. Like everything else, make the most of the good bits and minimize the bad bits. Take responsibility for making your life happy. Take responsibility for making your partner happy. Then just get on with it.

You must have heard of the book "Men are from Mars, Women are from Venus" by John Gray. I've never read it—it all sounded a bit tree huggy to me. But the same day I bought the book that saved my life by giving up drinking, I saw a subsequent book by Gray called

"Mars and Venus—together forever" and in a moment of weakness, bought it. (Surprisingly, this book also was in the bargain bin).

I read the giving up alcohol one first and gave up drinking. In my new found condition of permanent sobriety, I thought I'd give the Venus and Mars one a go. I was right the first time, it's a bit tree huggy but it explained a lot to me.

It explained why even after 3 marriages, I was still having the same problems with my third wife that I had with the previous two. The problem was not them but neither was it me! The problem actually is that men and women truly do speak different languages. Throw in some cultural chasms and, well, what did I expect?

In the same way that we are never taught how to manage money at school, neither are we taught how to manage our relationships and how to communicate with the opposite sex. The effects can be just as devastating.

Having read the book, I now understand why the things my partner says, make me so angry. I now know that I don't help anything by arguing and trying to set my partner straight. I know that its OK to not want to discuss things and just as OK to spend time doing mindless stuff that gives men so much satisfaction but drives woman crazy.

That was the good side of Greys book. But if you really become a devotee of his advice, you will spend the rest of your life trying to change everything you are, know and feel so that your partner (male or female) and you can communicate better. I'm sorry, I thinks thats a load of horse excrement. Try and understand each other, give it your very best shot, but life is too short to spend that much time on a relationship that requires you to be someone different to survive.

I have learnt not to take offence at apparent (or real) criticisms, not to feel under attack or defensive. This is just the way the conversation with your partner will go. Sometimes when everything has been said, it's appropriate to discuss the issues and come to some resolution. This is what men want to do immediately (find a solution) but I have learnt its better to just shut-up and listen. Solution time will come later. Sometimes my ego is a bit too bruised so instead of shouting and banging the table, I take time out (politely) and go do some man stuff, like play a game, hit some balls, go to the gym. When the heat has gone out of my head, a solution can always be found.

You must be true to yourself. Of course you should try and make a relationship work. Do your very best. However if making it work means being some-one you are not, just to please another person . . . . on your bike mate (or matess) and go try something else.

This is not sexist in anyway, despite being written from my male perspective. Be true to yourself, be clear about where you are going and then if people who have hitched themselves to your wagon don't want to go in the same direction, you owe it to them as well as yourself to cut them loose.

Again, its better not to give away a relationship if it can be repaired. Some of the advice given on repairing the mess though is just hilarious. Many times I have read that getting a boring relationship back on track involves scheduling a night of lust in advance! I can't think of anything less exciting than working late one night and checking the diary to find you have to rush home for a session of unbridled lust. Its just not going to happen. Better to schedule events that may (or may not) lead you both in that direction more naturally.

If you can start to rebuild the lost trust and communication, you have a stable platform on which to address all those differences that have been bugging your relationship for years. Some examples may include; different friends, different work attitudes, different dietary preferences, different ideas on fitness, even different life goals. For goodness sake you would need a book to list all the differences if you really tried. I suggest that you don't try!

All that is needed to address all these issues, is respect for the others opinion. Changing people's opinions is not going to happen. The best you can do is respect them.

I have come to the conclusion that love is not as its portrayed in the movies! Nor is it an on or off event. Its like an indicator on a stock chart. It has it ups and its downs. It can even go below zero (indicating hate I guess). But like all things in life (including the stock market) it goes up and down with time.

One of the reasons that I have been so quick to get out of marriages is that I have been desperately trying to avoid a loveless marriage. It seemed wrong to me that two people should stay together when they don't feel anything strongly for each other. What I didn't realize is that all relationships go through these ups and downs all the time. You can change the course of the chart. There is no inevitability about the chart only progressing downwards with time.

Marriage, any relationship . . . indeed life, is not the way it's supposed to be, it's the way it is. It's how you cope with it that makes the difference.

I do apologise if this section seems a bit unclear in its purpose—that's the way relationships are. I guess in summary I am exhorting you to try and make a reasonable relationship work. If you can't do that, here is how to exit.

Time to Leave

If after trying everything you still think its time to break up, here's how to tell if you have made the right decision. Be sure that you are in a sober, rational, unpressured and unemotional state of mind. Then make a clear, logical decision about what you think should happen.

This decision must be based on rational issues not emotion. Don't make a decision to leave to try and shock or hurt the other person. If you are hoping for that shock to lead to a change in behavior—prepare to be dissapointed. Understand that you must take responsibility for where the relationship is at present and that it is not someone else's fault. You got it here, now you need to fix it. If there have been years of attempts to improve things, attempts that failed, then nothing is likely to change it now.

Having made that clear headed decision, how do you feel? If you have decided to leave, it will have been a tough decision, one that's taken months or years. You will have invested plenty of emotional and financial capital into this relationship. There may be kids involved, dogs, and other things! There will be regret, sadness, but above all—if leaving is the right decision—there will be relief. The relief is intense, that huge chest heaving, deep sigh, kind of relief. If that's the feeling, get on with the next phase. If it's not, you will still feel confused and uncertain. In that case get back to fixing the mess up because you've made the wrong decision.

There are lots of reasons why things finally come to an end—it just life for a start! Nothing lasts forever. Maybe the catalyst is another party, maybe its money. Sometimes one or both of you have just run out of energy to continue the fight. Often one of you has fallen out of love—romantic talk for just got sick of it.

If you really can't fix it, the worst thing you can do is stay in a bad relationship. How many couples do you know where it the worlds worst kept secret that they are staying together "for the children". Somehow these people think that its good for the children to be bought up in a house with parents who can't stand the sight of each other and who spend most of their waking minutes arguing. Its better for the kids if the parents can mend things and stay together—that's certain. But if they can't, it is not good for the kids to go through the insecurity and unpleasantness created by a bad relationship.

Children want to feel stability and are remarkably resilient when it comes to how that stability is achieved. Because they are completely self-centered, a stable environment with the parents living apart can be just as satisfying for them as if you were together. I've checked with my own kids and I know that this is correct. But parents at war, either still living together or apart do not provide any sort of stability and the kids will suffer.

Even at this late stage, again I would advise trying to make the relationship work. Try taking responsibility for the state of the relationship rather than blame your partner. Complete honesty is often proscribed at this stage—something I would strongly advise **against**! Honesty is going to create an atomic explosion if things are going that badly already. Forget honesty and try humility. Listen to your partners gripes, do not take offence, say as little as possible and when forced, say what you know they want to hear. This is the way to diffuse explosive situations, not standing on your honour, defending your ego. Can the anger be taken out of this relationship?

If that answer is yes, then you can and should salvage the relationship, whether its just drifting around in a state of boredom or its in a more aggressive state of disrepair. If the answer is no, then you now have absolute confirmation that you should end the relationship before it poisons you both and all around you—including the kids, (if it hasn't already).

So you've done your best but its not enough . . . . here is how to get out properly.

Getting divorced the first time, is as daunting as buying your first house or learning how to trade stocks. In the same way, having done it once, it gets easier! I do not want to make divorce appear trivial, something that should be undertaken lightly. But if this is the best course open to you, I can confirm that it's not as bad as it's made out to be by those who get it wrong.

The first mistake made by most people deciding to exit a relationship is the amount of information sharing that goes on. Usually it's too much but either too much or too little are as bad as each other. It is insane to think that your life partner is going to become your *ex* life partner whilst remaining calm and cool about the whole deal—especially if it's not their idea! Both of you are going to feel rejected at some time and there is going to be a lot of emotion going around. While we want to be fair about this separation, its everyone for themselves from now on, so devise what I call an exit strategy and keep it to yourself.

The plan should include when and how the separation would ideally happen for you. This will include living arrangements, but especially how and when the financial split should occur. It may not pan out the way you plan it, but at least you will have a starting point for negotiations and having a plan helps prevent the inevitable emotional confusion that will arise.

Much avarice can arise over the separation of assets often in the name of securing "financial security" for your partner. Don't forget that financial security is also something with which you also need to be concerned. In any case, this division of assets often turns into a nasty vindictive exercise which can very easily be avoided all together by good planning.

During this planning phase and at all times from then onwards, ensure that the atmosphere is as happy and pleasant as possible. Don't argue, mutter under your breath, get angry or allow yourself feelings of anger or hurt. Its over, now you need to finish it nicely. After all, your aim is not to hurt the other person in any way. Your aim is to exit an unsatisfactory relationship in the best possible way so that you remain on excellent terms with each other and any kids involved.

As a starting point, the financial plan should involve an equal division of assets. By "assets" I mean your joint net worth. If you didn't have a statement of your joint net worth before, then you need one now at the planning stage. This is the sort of thing the bank will have asked for when you applied for a mortgage. It's a simple list of all the things you **own**, from which is deducted all the things you **owe**. The difference hopefully is positive and represents what you would be worth today if you sold everything you had and paid off all your debts. The trick here is not to forget something, like credit card debt or a personal loan.

Too often break ups focus just on **assets** not net worth. It is your joint net worth that needs to be divided up— assets **and** liabilities.

Your aim is to divide up your net worth, evenly. The same should be true of time with the kids (one week with one parent, one week with the other for example). From that starting point you make adjustments for deviations from equal division. If one partner is going to be the primary carer for the kids, how is that reflected in the division of assets? If one partner has no ability to earn income (really?), how is that reflected in the asset breakup?

Equal division of everything is the ideal, the starting point for discussion but such a situation will rarely ultimately prevail. Lets assume the worst—you are the primary income earner and your partner wants to have the kids full time. If this is your position set expectations low from the beginning with the "equal division" argument. Keep this going for a while then gradually start singing from a new song book!

In this situation, equal division is just a negotiating tactic. The reality is that your actual plan should include giving away just about everything to your spouse! What???

You heard correctly, plan to give your spouse the lions share of your assets. As an old friend of mine used to say . . . "its only money" and its not worth fighting over if you really want out. You move from "equal division" to "have the lot" slowly in small increments diffusing your partners anger and aggression at every step.

Like all life plans, your life after divorce needs to be funded. Figure out how much capital you need to support your anticipated life style as explained in section two. Then ensure that you obtain that much cash or assets easily converted to cash, in the separation. Give everything else away. It's just stuff!

Fighting like crazy over a car or a house that costs you money anyway is not sensible. If you think that half the assets are a genuinely fair deal, then go for half. Be prepared to settle for much, much less though. In the end what you need is a bit of cash. If you can also end up with somewhere to live, something to drive—heh that's a bonus.

So now we are down to dividing up the assets in a way that gives you the required amount of capital and leaves the rest to your (soon to be ex) spouse. Work on this division without anger, rancor, or the slightest bit of malice. Your aim is to be incredibly generous to avoid the whole thing developing into a battle royale . . . . specifically to avoid lawyers, and courts.

You do not want to avoid these wonderful institutions out of fear because you have nothing to fear. You want to avoid them to prevent the years of pain and suffering that the combative legal system is trained to initiate. Lawyers and courts cannot exist if there is no dispute. In your case you can write them and their associated massive cost, out of your relationship—if you handle everything well.

In summary be prepared to give your partner nearly everything. There are only two things you want: sufficient capital to generate enough monthly income to live your new life, and a guarantee of no ongoing alimony payments. Alimony payments (humorously called child support or child maintenance payments in Australia—the money goes to your ex, not the kids) are tantamount to financial death and are to be avoided at all costs! Cash flow is your requirement and the last thing you need is to be lumbered with a massive monthly debt before you even start earning income from your stock portfolio.

Just incase you are dealing with a psychopath (and you never know until the divorce) you might consider some insurance. The insurance I suggest is a small personal brokerage account held in the name of a very close and trusted friend. I am not suggesting something along the lines of a dodgy tax scheme. I am just suggesting spiriting a little away without your partner's knowledge during the divorce planning stage. If everything works out fine, you may want to throw this back into the joint pot for division. If not, and you do end up in court, then you will not be able to hide this account. However by giving your ex everything else (if necessary) the plan is to avoid legal scrutiny of your affairs thus keeping this little nest egg as a means of supporting yourself going forward.

The time it takes to build up this nest egg may determine your exit date. That's fine as long as you can keep the whole thing together till then.

I apologise to any of you who find this in some way distasteful or dishonest. However I have seen far too many divorces where the leaving party has been absolutely screwed, all because of insufficient planning. I repeat, I do not recommend exiting a relationship as the best or primary course of action. Usually things can be mended, albeit with a great deal of effort. However if the best way forward for you, after all things are considered is to separate from your spouse, you owe it to yourself and to your spouse and any kids, to plan it properly.

This strategy has a very high chance of allowing you to exit a toxic relationship with a friendship intact (critical if there are children involved) and with your financial future still sound. Isn't that the aim?

Kids

I have 6 children ranging from 28 years old to 6 years old at time of writing. All my friends thought I was crazy still having children at the age of fifty, but I fail to see the downside. Is it the cost? As explained in section two, I have that covered. Others have mentioned the fear of attending their son's 21st birthday party as a 71 year old! As explained under "Getting Fit", that doesn't worry me at all. In fact I intend to be more fit then, than now. Yet others think that they want to be doing what *they* want at this age (if they know what that is) instead of bringing up kids. Well bringing up kids **is** what I want.

Actually, in many ways, having children late in life is the best way to do it. When my first wife and I were having our family, we were struggling to make ends meet. The cost of disposable nappies was a strain on the weekly budget and we both had to work as well as look after the children. I traveled extensively and when I was at home there were a million and one maintenance jobs to do on and around our big old house.

Contrast that with today. I work from home. I see my youngest son and daughter every day and play an active role in their care and development. We live in a high rise apartment which does not require any of my time for maintenance. We are privileged to live in Singapore so we have live-in domestic help enabling us to do what we like with our time.

There is one downside to having babies late in life that should be mentioned. Its called broken sleep! I do not function well without sleep. The thought of waking every two hours as I did in the early days, did not enthrall me. As with everything else, there is an answer and I have to take this opportunity to heap praise on a wonderful woman whom I have never met, named Gina Ford.

My early parenting days were guided by principles like "never wake a sleeping baby" and "demand feeding". Ms Ford turns all that on its head in her fantastic book "The New Contented Little Baby Book". In essence, the idea is that a baby needs a certain amount of sleep and food. Just like adults, if they get that sleep during the day, they will not sleep at night. The same applies to food. If their intake is insufficient during the day, they will awake hungry at night. It just makes so much sense.

So if you do find yourself with babies later in your life (or any time really), I strongly advise reading Ms Fords book and sticking to the plan. My youngest son slept from 10:30pm till 7am from the time he came home from hospital and very quickly that moved to 7pm to 7am. We were told that was luck, but my youngest daughter (who is a very different personality) has stuck to the same schedule.

Mostly I have been a long distance father. Its not the best but you have to make the best of your situation. The only thing you can do is set a good example and I hope at least in some ways, I have done that. I am honoured by my friends who tell me that they have never seen such a close relationship as I have with my older children—so it is possible to achieve.

After the demise of my first marriage, I moved interstate but I saw my children at least 6 times a year. During one of these trips, I thought that I would try and leave some sort of lasting message with my children that would help them throughout their lives.

Its scary how these suggestions have worked out! I tried giving each of my kids responsibility for one of four important things in life. Each of them had to be all four, but each was responsible for ensuring one outcome for themselves as a model for everyone. That was nearly eighteen years ago or more and to my great delight (and surprise), it stuck!

The four things were:

- Be physically fit. You are nothing without your health. My eldest son, the biggest and strongest got this assignment. Today no-one is fitter.
- Look out for the family. My second son, the gregarious one was given this. To this day he keeps in touch with everyone (and has a delightful girlfriend who is even better at this). He is the glue!
- Make a lot of money. Without money you can achieve nothing in life for yourself or for others. My third son was given this challenge—he always had that look in his eye. At twenty four he already owns six (or maybe seven by now) rental properties and is well on his way to achieving financial freedom before he is thirty. He is truly dedicated.
- Be true to yourself. The final challenge was given to my then three year old daughter. Today no-one is more sure about who she is and where she is going. You can never be happy if you are living a lie.

I am really big on setting one line goals. When you write down a goal, even if you forget it, there is a magic that tends to make that goal happen often years later. Its somewhere in the subconscious and your actions tend to lead to that outcome. Exactly the same thing happened with the challenges I set my children.

The lesson I learnt from this is to be very careful with the messages we deliver to our kids. We are doing terrible damage to our children's senses through violent video games, through mindless hours of television watching and through the horrific pictures we see on the news.

Kids minds are numbed by horrors to which they are exposed and it is dangerous as well as unnecessary. I beg you to make every effort to fill children's lives with wonder and beauty so that the next generation may become the most elegant, charming, knowledgeable, and well educated people to populate the planet. Then and only then is there a chance for this earth and its future inhabitants.

Apart from all this, the best thing you can do when you do have children is to spend time with them—that's all that's needed. If you follow this plan to become financially independent then you will be able to do that—and everyone will benefit.

Surviving a Financial Crisis

In October 2007, just days after I put all my redundancy money into stocks, the market started a correction. A little rally followed that kept me and millions of others in the market, but unknown to all of us, this was the start of the most severe financial crisis the world has ever seen. For me personally, it was the start of five very tough years.

I did learn a great deal from that harrowing experience and I hope that by putting these lessons in writing, you can avoid the worst of what I had to go through when the next global or personal crisis hits.

1) In a crisis, CUT EXPENSES dramatically—especially any vices you may still have! For me, the response to a crisis is a good bottle of red. In truth I thought that $100 spent on wine would have no impact on the millions of dollars of margin calls I was trying to service. To see how untrue this is, just have a look at your next credit card bill. Even if there have been no especially big items, I am always surprised at the size of my monthly bill. The thousands of dollars I owe each month are not usually the result of a single large purchase. Rather the total is the sum of many small bills—dinners, wine, clothing etc. Small costs add up, so stop them if there is a crisis and take the chance to improve you fitness (if your small expenses are unhealthy ones like mine) as well as your bank balance.

2) To prevent heartbreaking calls in times of high demand for cash NEVER work on a margin account for your stocks. Let cash flow from property and stock trading, build up your capital. Its slower than using margin for sure, but you will never be faced with a margin call and if you have only purchased blue chips, their price will eventually recover.

3) NEVER expose yourself to currency risk. You cannot ever predict the direction or magnitude of currency fluctuations. A few very, very big players control these markets and they are so big that not even Governments can defend their currencies against them. A sudden (always unexpected) turn in the value of any currency can occur overnight at any time and can take

your fortune with it. I lost millions in the course of a week because of this exposure and I am not referring to paper losses. In times like this the banks convert your loans to the home currency and your debt increases by the amount that currency has been devalued. When I took out cross currency loans I was the smartest bloke in town! Suddenly I was the dumbest!

4) ALWAYS keep 6 months of living expenses in a cash reserve. It is very tempting to want to put that money to work in stocks or property but resist the temptation. Although you cannot foresee the event, there will be a time when you will be very glad you have that reserve.

Having a plan to avoid crisis is good and I strongly advise you to use something like my four rules above for that purpose. However, do not dwell on the negatives, the disasters that could occur, the worst case. Prepare for these events but then move on knowing that you are covered should the worst happen. This leaves your mind free to focus on your new Lifestyle and generating the income to fund it.

Superannuation

Governments have put a lot of money and effort into encouraging superannuation because they know that they are going to run out of money to fund the baby boomers retirement.

Super is not a bad idea, its just that you are forced to put it in the hands of incompetent companies who earn very little on it and charge you a fortune each year whether you make money or not.

Four years ago, I received the latest return from my Superannuation plan run by the largest such organization in Australia. They managed to **lose** 6.16% on the sum I had invested with them over the previous 12 months. That's right, while they as a company announced a massive profit for the year (albeit slightly smaller than the previous year) I suffered a 6.16% loss. The agent who answered my irate call, explained that this was due to the poor performance of property and Australian and International shares over the period. However, in the same period and under the same conditions, I was able to achieve a return of 30% trading stocks. What is wrong here?

Whats wrong is that big businesses are not the best "people" to be looking after your money. Only you care about your money and only you should be looking after it. If you have been forced to take out super then OK, consider it a sort of forced saving but don't add to it despite the apparently attractive tax treatment of such finds. Paying less tax on low or negative returns is not much good!

Educate yourself in how to make money with cash positive properties and trading stocks and take responsibility for your own financial future. You will do a lot better than any company charged with making a profit while they mishandle your super.

Get a Job

You need to get a job for a lot of reasons. Self-esteem, confidence and socializing are just as important as money. But make no mistake, you need the money! The second part of this book explains all about money and how to fund "retirement" (by which I mean not working for someone else) before you are thirty. The last part "Putting it all Together" explains how to exit your job—and get a redundancy payout. However to begin with, you need a job.

As detailed below in the Making Money section; no matter what the job, become the absolute best. You want to shine, to stand out. You want to be the first person the bosses think of when promotions are coming round. Be pleasant, honest and above all hard working. Get a job doing something you really love which makes doing well at it that much easier. Even if you don't know that you are going to love it, most jobs are OK. Just get really good at it.

The aim of this phase of your life is to climb the corporate ladder as fast as you can. "But I'm not a corporate person" I hear you say. "I hate the politics; I just want to get the job done". WRONG. You are doing this job for a different reason to just about everyone else in the company.

Most employees are doing a job just to survive. Because they see no way out, they blame the work. They have not learned to take responsibility for where they find themselves in life.

You are doing this job for an entirely different reason. This job is going to give you the means to stop working for someone else before you reach thirty years old. You may have only been in the "workforce" for ten or so years by then. To achieve that goal, you need to be the best employee there is and get promoted to the highest position possible as fast as possible.

In the end, I will explain how you can be made redundant at a time of your choosing. Redundancy payouts are based on your salary—not any other benefits. You want that payout to fund your stock trading business and to pay down property, so you must be in the highest paying position that the company has before you take that option.

There is no reason you can't be the Managing Director of your company. I promise you that the MD is no smarter than you. In many cases he is where he is through "luck". Luck is something that works in your favour when you have a plan and a sense of urgency.

So take it upon yourself to get bumped up through the company hierarchy as fast as you can. This is critical to your life plan so take no prisoners. Step on toes if you have to—who cares if you upset some people. The bosses want to promote people who want to be promoted! They want people with a killer instinct and that all important sense of urgency.

Get started on this plan now—its vital.

Education

Education is not a guaranteed path to success any more. There are as many unemployed graduates as anyone else out there today. In any case, you can most definitely achieve your goals with any level of education. However, life is about acquiring knowledge. An enquiring mind thirsts for answers and formal education is one way to find them.

Keep learning always. Study fulltime if you like before you start work, or part time after. Learn about the things that interest you and you become a more interesting person. Interesting people are surrounded by other interesting people and that's what makes life . . . . well . . . . interesting!

As with everything in life is you choose to undertake a degree for example, don't settle for average results. Be the dux of the class, the faculty, the Uni. Don't do stuff by half—ever. But undertake whatever level of education that you choose, for the love of the subject, not because it will get you a better job or more money—it won't.

I referred earlier to the 70% of law students who undertook their study purely because they thought it would result in a higher paying job than any alternative degree! I fear that the same applies to many professionals in whom we must sometimes put our trust. Don't fall for that trap. Learn about what you love—and find a lawyer or any professional from the 30% who **do** love their subject.

PART TWO

MAKING MONEY

The Two Sources of Wealth

Ignorance is the source of all evil. If there is one evil for which my generation must take responsibility, it's that of the financial ignorance of our kids. However, with the internet there is really no excuse for ignorance of anything so take your share of the responsibility and educate yourself . . . . fast.

Financial independence is a very simple matter, crucial to a successful life yet its not taught in schools in any realistic way. Ignorance of even simple finance allows the development of a financial industry which is almost criminal in its exploitation of the masses. In my experience, much of the finance industry is incompetent at best and most certainly have their own interests rather than yours, at heart.

The trouble is that ignorance breeds fear and not wanting to look stupid, people accept the rubbish that the industry feeds them. Take my pet hate—"negative gearing". Negative gearing is a term that every man woman and child in Australia pretends to have great knowledge about. Mention it anywhere and everyone present will nod sagely—"Ah yes negative gearing". It is so well accepted that it is rarely if ever questioned. It is one of the great fallacies perpetuated by the financial industry (especially accountants) because it makes them money.

Please be very clear, negative gearing is a fancy word for losing money! That's all it is, losing money. The ridiculous concept is that its OK to lose money (say with an investment property) because you can offset that loss by paying less tax on other income such as salary. Naturally you will be spending some of that tax "saved" on accountants to put your ever more complex tax return together—but that's tax deductible too!

There is much that is wrong with this thinking mainly the fact that every week your losing property will cost you money. No matter what fancy footwork the accountant does at the end of the year, it will have cost you cash every week to fund your losing property. And yes I know there is a clever way that you can claim the loss each quarter but that's still not the point.

What happens when you leave that secure source of income and you aren't able to claim the loss against something else? Getting more and more involved in complex plans is not a good idea. Losing money on investments is not a good idea. Better to get right out of the tax dodging mindset and instead set out at all times to make more money. Paying tax means you are making money. Pay up and shut up and keep making money. If you get your three flags working tax won't bother you anyway.

And so to the two sources of wealth, the heading of this section. There are only two ways to increase your wealth and they are Capital Gains and Cash Flow. Both are generated by assets.

A capital gain is made if you purchase an asset and at some time in the future you sell it for more than you paid. Please note here that you only make that gain when you sell—not because the asset is simply valued at more than you paid for it. I make this distinction because again, parts of the financial industry will try and get you to buy assets (like shares) and then tell you in their quarterly report that you have made money because the value of the shares has gone up. Nonsense! You have made nothing at all unless you sell the shares.

Lets not get into the various dubious reasons behind them making this erroneous statement. Just understand that there is no profit if you have not sold the asset, just a pretend or imaginary "paper" gain. Never allow a financial company to charge you for imaginary gains.

Cash flow as the name suggests, is just the movement of cash. It can be positive or negative. When you buy something, cash flows out of your hands and in to someone else's. If you have bought true assets, the cash they generate will be greater than the cash it costs to keep them. Robert Kiyosaki of Rich Dad Poor Dad fame, describes assets as ONLY those things which generate positive cash flow for you. By this description, the house you live in for example is NOT an asset. It costs you plenty but doesn't generate any income. On this point I agree with Mr K.

If you are working for someone to generate a salary, then its your time that is the income earning asset. If you buy something that you lease out and the cash coming in is greater than the cash out, that asset is earning you cash.

Some assets (like investments properties) can generate both capital gains and positive cash flow. However the recent global financial crisis has shown that asset values are often not quite what they seem! All sorts of asset classes—especially property have turned out not to be worth anything near what they were valued at just a few months before.

My strong advice then is to completely disregard the possibility of potential capital gain (at least in the short term). It may or may not eventuate. If it does, then you are in a bonus situation! Calculate the value of any potential asset purchase purely on its cash flow generation.

By separating the two classes of income (capital gains and cash flow) you will demystify any potential investment that you make. Never confuse the two and never place any value on what someone tells you something may be worth in the future. Past performance has absolutely nothing to do with the future. Only make investments based on their ability to increase your wealth through positive cash flow right now.

Here is an example of the difference between capital gain and cash flow and how people get them confused. The greatest investor of all time and one of the worlds richest people is the well know Warren Buffet. His strategy for generating wealth is supposed be one of capital gains. He buys companies that he determines are undervalued and waits for them to increase in value. He says his time horizon for holding stocks is "forever".

Dennis Wall

It's a simple plan that appeals to many but wait a minute! If he buys stocks and never sells them, his net worth may well increase but what does he use for cash to buy a hamburger? To buy food, clothes, and every other essential you need CASH. Now Mr Buffet is no dummy so the assets he buys not only increase in value over time, they pay him dividends which is CASH every quarter. That's only one of the ways that his assets generate cash (others include the use of options which we will look at later).

Most people just accept that Mr Buffets strategy is capital gains and by inference then this is a good strategy for them! They don't look for the cash flow. Always look for the cash flow. The only thing that you can genuinely calculate before you buy an asset is cash flow. You cannot buy a meal or a tank of fuel with theoretical capital gains. Only cash will pay the bills and excess cash (above living expenses) will allow you to make more cash positive investments.

ONLY MAKE CASH POSITIVE INVESTMENTS—treat capital gains as a bonus.

The negative gearing phallacy (intentional spelling mistake) relies on confusion of the two sources of wealth. The assumption made by the Realtor, the Accountant and many other finance industry professionals, is that the capital gain will eventually offset the negative cash flow of a property. Well maybe, but maybe not.

Some will tell you "never sell an investment property". If its cash positive, contributing to your growing wealth every single week, why would you ever sell it? It depends on where you are in your Lifestyle plan. In the early years while you are working and trying to maximise debt, it's true, don't sell properties. Later when you are at the generating income phase (retiring) you need to sell to pay down debt. More on that later.

Be aware that when you do sell properties, you will be liable for capital gains tax. Once more I remind you making money (and therefore paying tax) is good.

Always be clear if any proposed investment is a capital gains or cash flow play. Don't allow the two to be confused. Separate them completely and then disregard completely the capital gains story!

The General Financial Plan

What you want is to own lots of assets that earn you money while you sleep. This is called passive income. If that's all you have though, your lifestyle is going to be limited. You also need to be able to generate lots of additional cash, regularly, without the need to spend too much time doing that. If you can do both those things you will be truly financially independent. You can do exactly what you choose to do, live how you choose to live and "retire" if you so choose.

Here's how to do that before you are thirty:

Get into as much debt as you can afford to service as a youth, to buy as many properties as possible. As a rule of thumb 20 is a good number but much depends on their value and the age at which you want to stop working for someone else. The properties should always be cash positive, meaning rent received exceeds all outgoings including mortgage repayments (principle and interest or P&I) if only by a small amount. Take P&I because you want to be paying down the debt—not by a huge amount but you do want to be paying it down. If you are doing this young, then you have a long, long time to pay back the principal so it won't be much anyway on a monthly basis.

Use as little of your own cash as possible to build up this portfolio. You do that by using the equity built up in earlier properties as the deposit to borrow more. This is usually possible after you have owned two or three properties for a few years. This is a great way to access any capital gain without having to sell the properties.

Since all properties will be cash positive, you will soon be generating reasonable quantities of spare cash. This is your spending money. If you can save some, put this cash to work generating more cash from trend trading stocks.

Purchase non incoming earning assets (like boats and cars) only from the cash generated through either the properties or stocks. Use any savings from salary as a deposit to buy more houses. Once you have reached your target number of properties, build up the assets in your stock portfolio until your target monthly income is being generated.

Since the properties are cash positive there is no value in further reducing the debt beyond the P&I payments until you are ready to leave your job. Debt that is generating income is nothing to be afraid of; in-fact it is something to actively chase! As you pay down the debt, your portfolio of properties will start to produce you even more cash. Cash just keeps rolling in from these two generally unrelated sources of income—property and stocks.

How simple is that? What's more, it really is as simple as it sounds.

You will be selling some of the properties as you approach your planned retirement date, to pay off the others. That's how you calculate how many properties you need. Lets just say you want $4,000 a month income. You can achieve that with only four properties that have no debt and are generating $250 each a week in rent. Properties like that probably cost you less than $200,000 when you bought them. If you have 80% debt on them, you need to pay down $640,000. That would require another four properties of the same value.

So if you only needed $4,000 a month, all you need is 8 properties worth $200,000 with 80% debt to retire! Need more like $8,000 a month—that's 16 properties and so on.

That's the general outline and now I will explain the two strategies in more detail.

Property

Have you ever heard real estate agents going on about the return on property? They give you numbers like 5% or 8% and look at you as though you should be impressed. To this extent, real estate agents can be considered as part of the financial industry and therefore not always acting in your best interests. They are using jargon to confuse the ignorant in order to procure a sale—don't listen.

They calculate this return by dividing the rental income from a property by the total purchase price. Often they neglect to deduct the costs from the income and just use a nice big gross number to inflate the supposed return. In any case, the return they are talking about has no meaning. You would be better off putting your money in the bank for these sorts of returns.

Do you intend to pay cash for the full price of the property? I hope not, that would be a very poor use of the leverage available to you through mortgages. The only number you care about is the amount of cash (after all costs are deducted) that this property will add to your bank account, divided by the amount of cash you put down on the property. This is referred to as the cash on cash return. If you look at it this way, the correct way, you will find that you can make amazing returns on property.

To begin this strategy you will need enough cash for a deposit, and a level of income that can demonstrate to a bank that you can make the repayments on a mortgage. The best way to do this is to get a job.

As noted in "Get a Job", almost any job will do but it's much better to find one that you like, since you will be doing it for the next 5 to 10 years. Also it's better to stay with the one job and progress through the ranks as fast as you can than to chop and change around. People change jobs to improve their career—thinking they will be working for 40 years or more. By all means choose a career that you like, but you are doing this to implement your lifestyle strategy so enjoy whatever you get into because you won't be doing it for long!

Progressing through the ranks of a company is very easy. All you have to do is stand out from the crowd, impress people. In Australia that's so easy it's laughable. Just turning up on time will do it! Be reliable, honest and hardworking and you will shine above 99.9% of all employees. Most employees hate what they are doing, see no future, turn up late (if they turn up at all) and can't wait to knock off. That's because they have no plan of any sort and certainly no financial plan.

You are different. Implement your plan and enjoy the job that is helping you achieve it.

Then learn to budget. Again budgets are simple. The amount you spend needs to be less than you earn. The less you spend, the more you save. The more you save, the quicker you can start your financial strategy. See, simple!

Budgeting doesn't mean being boring, staying at home and watching TV. It just means if you can only afford to go out once or a week, then only go out once a week. Find something else to do on the other nights, like improve your education, learn to trade, look for properties, or get fit. The priority is financial independence. Once you have that, you can go out as often as you like.

While you're saving for the deposit, you can start the search for a cash positive property—and that takes time because amazingly, I've never seen a property advertised as cash positive. Usually you have to **make** a property cash positive.

There are three ways to make a property cash positive. First, buy it at a very low price. Second get very good rent for it and third, borrow at the lowest interest rate you can.

Price seems obvious but it isn't. As is often said, you make your money when you buy a house not when you sell it. You must negotiate and although this is not an Australian habit it can make you a lot of money. To get a good price, you need a motivated seller—one who really needs to sell for some reason. You need to look at lots of properties and ask lots of questions to find motivated sellers (since they rarely advertise that fact either).

Don't be arrogant in your negotiations ("take this price or leave it") and don't be rude or aggressive. Just find a seller who has a bit more pressure on them than most. Maybe they are going through a divorce, can't meet their mortgage commitments, lost their job or need to move interstate. If they are not motivated, move on. This is a numbers game. If you ask enough partners for a dance, one will finally say yes!

There are reams of books written about this game and you can read them if you like but like everything else, once you strip away the rubbish and the vested interests, it's pretty easy. If you ask, you will easily find out what rent the property will probably achieve. Ask the agent about the costs like rates, water, body corporate (if strata title). Ask the bank what the monthly cost of the mortgage will be (with the minimum deposit possible). Add your costs together and convert them to a weekly rate and there you have it! If the likely rent doesn't exceed the costs, you can either: negotiate a lower purchase price to reduce the loan, find a way to increase the rent, find a cheaper loan or find another deal.

Assuming you have negotiated a good price, then you also want to maximize the rental income. Small and low cost additions or alterations can make a significant improvement to the rental return on any property. Sometimes you only need five or ten dollars a week to make a property cash positive.

Almost always, there are improvements that can be made to bathrooms and kitchens and these are very cheap and easy to do yourself. A new fridge, a coat of paint, bench tops, new floor coverings (especially getting rid of the shag pile in the toilet) and a host of other little things all make a place much more desirable. Think about it yourself, if the bathroom and kitchen are nice, would you pay an extra five or ten dollars a week? I bet you would. Often a weekend's work will be all that's required. There's something you can do with the nights that you are not going out!

Generally speaking first time investors make the mistake of looking for something to buy that they can ultimately live in themselves. Don't make that mistake. Maybe you will live in it for a while (like six months to get a first home buyers grant if that still exists) but that's not why you are buying. You are buying for a long term, cash positive investment.

These are most often found in the less desirable suburbs. Near Universities are great, inner city is good and certainly near public transport and shops. I have been called a slum landlord by friends who like to buy in "better areas" but I know who makes the best return. Generally go for apartments (less maintenance) with one or two bedrooms that can be easily let out for a cash positive return.

Never leave a property vacant—that's the surest way to turn a property cash negative. If for any reason there is a problem letting a place out, drop the rent immediately but sign a short term lease. It is much better to be getting less for a short while than to be getting nothing. Find out why it's not getting the price you want. Are there outstanding maintenance issues? Fix them immediately and get back into the black as soon as possible.

Don't rule out commercial properties. Commercial can make fantastic investments as long as business sentiment in the area is OK. They can be harder to let in times of economic downturn but retail space in high traffic areas is always in high demand. Warehousing can also be excellent.

The advantage of commercial is that the tenant is responsible for all repairs, renovations and bills. You usually have to look after services to the property including power, water, air-conditioning and heating as well as roofing and other structural issues, but the rest is up to the tenant. Just do the numbers and if its cash positive then why not?

The best way to ensure that you have great tenants in commercial or residential (who also pay high rent) is to be an outstanding landlord. Get things fixed fast, do what you say you will do and be fair and reasonable. As with everything else in life, treat others the way you would like to be treated. For goodness sake employ a good agent to look after them for you. They have a bigger pool of tenants than you can ever hope to access, they take all the hassle out of the whole thing and of course their cost is a tax deduction.

The third way to make a property cash positive is to borrow cheaply. In Australia, there is little you can do about the interest rate that you pay. The four major banks collude on interest rates (though this is illegal in every other area of commerce). However you can (and should) look hard at the many other costs which are very negotiable. Ask them to explain all their costs and keep asking until you are satisfied. There are fees for every single part of the transaction from drawing up the mortgage (as if it isn't a standard document!) to the ludicrous cost of paying out the loan early. See which ones they will drop or reduce. This all adds up and the more you can save, the more you have to put toward your next property.

Dennis Wall

Despite the arrogant attitude of all the banks, remember that you are the customer and you have a right to ask questions and a right to choose if the deal they are offering is the best for you. Exercise your rights.

One way that sometimes comes up to avoid high Australian interest rates, is to borrow overseas. This is probably not an option open to you but if it does arise, run the other way as fast as you can! Foreign exchange risk is not worth taking no matter how rosy it seems at the time. Always borrow in the same currency as the income from that asset. If you are buying Australian investment properties, then always borrow in Australia. If you are buying overseas then always borrow in that currency. Do I sound like someone that learnt that lesson the hard way? Dead right.

The only time that you can break this rule is if you only borrow 50% or less of the debt in a foreign currency. This should be enough to protect you from the huge swings possible in the Forex markets—maybe not in another GFC but generally speaking 50% is safe.

I mentioned earlier that you should have as much debt as you can afford to service. When I speak of maximizing debt I refer to **safe** debt. There is a great book by Ken Fischer called "The only three questions that count", which gives a really good perspective on safe debt. In summary Fischer contends that if you can borrow money at a rate that is lower than you can earn by investing it, you have a moral obligation to yourself and your family, to borrow as much as you can! This is an incredibly simple concept often completely ignored.

If you can borrow money at a lower cost than you can earn by investing it, you should borrow as much as you can.

The safety of the debt is the key and again it's linked to the two different sources of wealth—capital gains and cash flow. If for some reason you are unable to pay your mortgage, you may have to sell a house to pay back the loan. If this happens at a time when the value of properties is depressed there may be a capital loss and you get less for the property than you owe—now you are in trouble. This happened to many house holders in the US and was the cause of the first round of the Global Financial Crisis in 2007/2008.

However, if you have purchased properties which are truly cash positive, this cannot happen to you! Cash is King. If the rent is paying all costs and leaving some spare cash, you cannot be at risk of borrowing too much. Unless interest rate go crazy or rents collapse (and these things can happen) you are safe. To minimize the risks, you should fix the interest rate for as long as you can and you should not borrow to the absolute maximum the bank will allow.

When you fix interest rates, there will certainly be times when the variable rate is lower and your friends will be paying less interest than you. Big deal. This is about certainty of cash flow. If the property is cash positive at the fixed rate, then fix it. You will never need to worry about rates going up.

If the bank will allow you to borrow 90% of the value of a property, consider if you can afford 80%. For the first few properties you probably will not be able to find the extra cash, so borrow the maximum but be sure to take out a P&I loan (principle and interest). You are paying back part of the debt every month as well as the interest with this type of loan. This makes you less vulnerable every month to an interest rate hike. P&I makes it a bit harder to find a cash positive property though so bear all that in mind when you are looking for a property.

Like most things, the first investment property is the hardest. You have to organize lawyers, building inspections, find a rental agent, set up a mortgage and plenty of other things. I am always amazed at how complex it is and how many professionals have to be involved just to buy a little house! You can spend ten times that amount on stocks with the click of a button, not a lawyer in sight—but that's the way it is.

You will also have to deal with less motivated mates telling you that it's not worth all the hassle, asking you to come out and have a drink instead of painting a bathroom and other distractions. I guess they mean well but understand that they are acting out of ignorance. These are the same people that in years to come will view your success with envy and say that you were just lucky! There is no luck involved in your financial success—just hard work and dedication. You will just have to battle through the first time. Thereafter it becomes easier and easier. Don't give up. Don't be afraid to ask questions and call in favours.

Stocks

Stocks are a tiny bit more complicated than property in terms of your own education. Other than that it is much simpler to make (and lose) money from the stock market than from property. Like everything, stocks are a bit daunting until you look into them and find that the truth is far less complex than the "experts" would have you believe.

Once you know how to make money from money—you will be hooked! Not only is it fun, its relatively easy and can be done anywhere there is an internet connection—like on a boat. The only tool you need is your laptop/tablet. Its also a very cool way to make a living since most people have no idea what you do but they assume that you have some magical powers that normal humans do not! That's all nonsense of course although I encourage that line of thought as a bit of an ego trip! Being able to make money from money is about education, nothing more.

For me, stocks are about generating cash. However, many people find the whole concept so daunting that they just can't get started. If you are one of those people, there is a really very easy way to begin trading stocks. This is a capital gains strategy rather than cash flow but it will give you practice at trading, practice at charting and increase your wealth without even trying! The method is called Dollar Cost Averaging.

Find a stock you like, any stock. It might be the company you work for, a friend or family member works for or just a company whose products you like. It can be listed in the US or Australia. Work out how much money you can spare each month—it really doesn't matter how much but the more the better of course.

Each month, buy that dollar amount of shares in the company you have chosen. That's it. By using the same amount of money each month, you automatically buy more when the stock is cheap and less when the stock is more expensive. Consequently the average dollar price you pay per share (the dollar cost average) declines all the time.

Now that you own a stock, you will have more interest in following its price chart and then you can start to apply everything below with a bit more than passing interest! Give it a go—its fool proof and an effortless way to start if you are new to stocks.

My first foray into stocks was as a long term, Buffet style investor. When these returns proved a bit slow (and lacked cash flow) I moved to day trading. When I lost as much money as I could stomach at that game, I learnt how to use options in a strategy called "covered calls". I loved this strategy so much that I taught it as well as practiced it for years, believing this to be the true and perfect way to make money from the market. Maybe it was just bad timing but although I could generate income, the value of the portfolio kept declining—no good in the long run.

As it turns out, there is no perfect way to make money out of the market that works all the time. That's because the market is an ever-changing beast. The "market" reflects the collective psychology of the millions of players who range from multibillion dollar fund managers to retail investors like us. It also reflects all known information about all 15,000 listed companies as well as a good dose of rumour and speculation about many of these companies. As you might guess, finding a universal strategy that fits all possible situations that can arise is very difficult.

In the end I have reverted to the most simple of strategies—buy low, sell high (and the reverse by shorting stocks). I think if you can master the technical analysis and the trading discipline required, this is the safest way to make good returns. However there is room for multiple strategies and here is how I now apply them.

Financial markets in general and the stock market in particular, tend to run in reasonably well defined patterns. These are tracked by charts of an index or of an individual stock. As Dr Alexander Elder states in his outstanding book "Come into my Trading Room", a successful trader doesn't try and make sense of all the market complexity. They just look for common patterns that emerge time after time.

The first pattern to recognize is that known as Stages or Phases. (I will use the terms interchangeably, but be aware that the term "phases" usually references Elliot Wave moves which are a little similar, but more complex than my use of "stages").

All markets and indeed individual stocks, go through four stages that can be thought of as a forward leaning "S" or / shape. Stage one is the bottom of the "S". It is the period of consolidation that occurs as a downtrend ends. At this stage stocks are often referred to as "bouncing along the bottom". Here is a good time to employ the strategy of writing covered calls with a small percentage of capital also used to trade stocks on the long side.

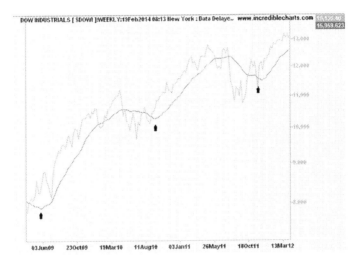

This is a 3 year weekly chart of the DOW with the 20 period moving average (smoother line) added. The overall shape I am referring to is quite nicely shown on the moving average line between the black arrows.

The same pattern keeps on occurring in all time frames and it is recognising that which allows us to make some money from the market.

Stage two is the upward sloping back of the / shape. Here stocks are steadily rising in price and depending on the slope of this rise, it's a great time to put emphasis on traditional long trading of stocks—buying and holding until they turn. It is also safe to be using covered calls in this stage but you limit your upside so best to just swing trade stocks especially if the curve is steep.

After some time, the rally will run out of steam and stock prices enter a period where they are "bouncing along the top". This is stage 3, the top of the "S". Here there is a strong risk of the market or stock coming crashing down—although we don't know when. At this stage if still going long, you need tight stops and you can start to sell short.

At stage 4, the market has turned from the top and has begun a decline. At this stage the focus is almost entirely on shorting stocks to benefit from price declines.

A word about shorting and buying puts. Usually I advise against opening a brokerage account which allows margin—ie allows you to borrow to buy stocks and options. You should never, ever, EVER borrow to trade anything. The risk is far too high. The problem is that in a cash account (that is non-margin) you cannot sell short.

Selling short is exactly the same as going long—but in reverse. When you go long, you buy a stock with the expectation that it will rise in value. After it does, you sell. If it doesn't, you use an automatic stop loss to kick you out before you lose too much.

When you think a stock is going to drop in price, you can sell it before you own it (sell short) expecting to buy it back later at a cheaper price. You are effectively borrowing this stock from the broker. If the stock does not decline, you use an automated stop loss to buy it back at a price which prevents you from losing too much.

If you don't run a margin account the broker will not allow you to sell short. Then the only way that you can profit from a stock declining is to buy a Put. When a stock declines in price, the value of a Put against that stock increases in value. So you buy a Put and sell it later at a higher price. You would buy a Put that is two or three months out and that is "at the money". They are cheap relative to the stock so you can buy lots, and they move in price rapidly so you can make lots too! Because you own the option, there is no risk of being called.

Problem is, they move the other way just as fast and you can't set stop losses on them so you can lose a fortune while you sleep! Not a good idea. The other thing is that options (of which Puts are one type) are not like stocks—they have a finite life. The value of an option is determined by the stock price, the time till expiration, volatility and interest rates. Every day, they lose a little bit of value as they get closer to the time when they expire. I have lost money when a stock did move downwards but the Put I bought went down in value even so! That's the danger of time value. My advise? Selling short is safer than buying Puts.

Back to Market Phases. Each of the phases or stages can last for variable periods of time and there is no merit in trying to pick where one stage has finished and the next started. You will only know that in hindsight. The point is to know the stage you are in now and select an appropriate strategy to make money.

When referring to stocks by the way, I am only talking about the US stock market. I know that the timing is a bit awkward if you are in Australia, but the US is the biggest market in the world by a long shot and you need that size (liquidity) to be able to make money reliably. However, the same principles described below apply to any market so if you prefer to trade Oz then no problem.

That's the general plan, now I will go into everything in a bit more detail.

You know how stocks work. A stock or share is an actual part (a share) of a company. If things go well for the company, the stock price should go up, and the opposite if things go badly. In practice, there are many things that can be unrelated to the company's performance, that affects its share price, but that's the theory.

Everyone has an opinion about the direction of the stock market! Regardless of age, gender or profession, most people will be happy to re-tell what they have read in the papers about the future direction of the market. Its incredible with so much information today, that there can be so many different views possible. And actually every one of these opinions is correct! If your Granny thinks the market is going to collapse—she is right. If the Postman thinks its going to rally—he is right. The question is . . . . when? The market has one constant—it moves. These moves can be up, down or sideways. It makes these moves in all time frames be that minutes, hours, days, months or years.

You need to know what your time frame is and how to identify if a stock is likely to make a strong move within that time-frame.

Four Little Secrets to Making Money in the Stock Market:

1. select your time frame,
2. understand the trend within that timeframe,
3. select the appropriate trading strategy and then
4. stick to the rules.

Always follow these secrets and you will make money— guaranteed. If you deviate at all, even the slightest little bit, I promise you the market will murder you. Lets go through each little secret in detail.

The first little Secret: Select the Time Frame

What time frame should you use? Do we want to look at stock movements in the short, medium or long term, and anyway what do these terms mean?

Our intention from trading is different to many others. We are not in this game to steadily build up wealth so that someday we can retire—we use our property portfolio for that. We are in this game to make money now so that we can retire now! That means we want to generate cash on a weekly (or at most monthly) basis, in order to live. So now we know that our time frame is between 5 to 10 trading days, maybe up to 20 days maximum (roughly one trading month). That puts us in the category of "swing" or "short term trend" traders. I use the 5 to 10 day time frame but allow stocks that continue to move in the right direction, up to 20 days before making my exit.

Having a defined time frame helps you to understand the sort of analysis you want to undertake when deciding which stocks you want to use to trade.

The Warren Buffets of the world use extensive fundamental analysis of a company. This is a good idea if you have a very long time frame and your primary aim is capital gain. It involves painstaking review of annual reports, financial reports, products, customers and management (among other things) to determine the true current and future value of a company and therefore when the current share price is a bargain and should be purchased.

Our time frame of 5 to 10 days is much shorter than this and our aim is cash flow rather than long term capital gain. As noted, in the short term many factors external to the company can have a huge impact on its share price—including if the US Federal Reserve Chairman (currently Janet Yellen) coughs or pauses at an inopportune time in one of her many presentations to the US Senate! Its hard to analyse the mass hysteria that characterizes market moves on many occasions in this way.

If fundamentals are your bag however, the financial wizards at Yahoo Finance have made it all a lot easier with a number they call a "Stock Scouter Rating" which can be found at moneycentral.msn.com/investor/StockRating. This rating takes into account just about all possible factors including comparing the company to its peers. A stock with a rating of 1 means you should run away. A rating of 10 is an outstanding company. I used to make use of this rating in the selection of stocks to use for writing covered calls. If it makes you feel better you can check this number when you find an otherwise good stock. However over our time frame, whether a companies fundamentals are good or not, you can still make money from the stock. For swing trading, there is no substitute for the second type of analysis—Technical Analysis.

Technical analysis is about looking for patterns in the charts. Charts are the footprints of money. They track without emotion, the actual prices of a stock over time. Depending on how you want to view the charts you can look at the closing price (line chart) or the open, high, low and closing price (OHLC) for the day. You can present the information in different ways like line, candle sticks (my personal favourite) or point and figure charts. They can be viewed in any time frame you choose.

Stock prices cannot lie! If you have ever read a company report you will quickly see the "spin" that can be put on everything. Lets not call this version of events a lie, but any event in a company's life can be presented in many different ways. Stock prices do not suffer from this problem. Every closing price represents the markets opinion of all events that are known or even guessed at, at that time. This is the true value of the stock price.

The only way to make consistent money in the market is to have a thorough knowledge of technical analysis or charting. You need to read as much as you can on this topic but you must read the book I mentioned above— "Come into my Trading Room" by Dr Alexander Elder. He presents a variety of alternative ways to look at stocks and indicators to use. I will address a few of the most important indicators as we go through the rest of the secrets.

Since our time frame is a few days to a month, you will need to use a chart with daily prices and a time frame of say one to 6 months. The actual time span will depend on which chart makes the most sense to you. Sometimes lines of support and resistance are only obvious with a 6 month time frame. Just flick around until the you find the one that is most clear to you. Usually I toggle between a 6 month and a 2 month candlestick chart for the daily charts.

I borrow heavily from Doctor Elders idea of also using a weekly chart (where each bar represent the price range of the week) to make decisions about a stock. I use one with two years of data. I talk about how to use these charts in the next secret.

The Second Little Secret: Understand the Trend

The next thing to do is check the phase of the market and the individual stock you are interested in. Stocks can move independently of the broader market but if they are in line, you have that much better chance of identifying a reliable pattern.

I use the Dow Jones Industrial Average ($DJIA is the ticker in most charting programs) to tell me where the top 30 companies in the US are going. Where they go, there go most of the others! Is the market in stage 1, 2, 3 or 4? This will help you determine if you are looking for stocks to buy, sell short or sell covered calls against.

Within each phase, stocks continue to move in a jagged pattern either up, down or sideways—there are no other alternatives. If a stock is in an uptrend it is making higher lows and higher highs. In a downtrend, it makes lower lows and lower highs as it bounces along. In a sideways move, the highs and lows seem to be stuck between a line of resistance you can draw across the highs and a line of support that it can't appear to break that you can draw under the lows.

However they never make these moves in a straight line, they bounce around, making it difficult to spot the trend. Its easier to insert an indicator called a moving average to make a smooth line that can quickly tell you the trend at a glance.

Add a 22 period exponential moving average (22 EMA) to both the weekly and daily chart. If this line is heading up, you are in an uptrend. If heading down . . . . a downtrend and yes, if drifting along more or less flat, you are in a horizontal or sideways trend.

Although our time frame is 5 to 10 days, the bigger picture is always important and you must make you decision to enter a position based on three trends (in this order):

1. the phase of the broader market
2. the trend of the weekly chart
3. the trend of the daily chart

Its very possible to only look at the daily chart, and identifying what looks like a roaring uptrend, decide to go long. Within a couple of days the stock has collapsed and you are stopped out with a feeling of shock and amazement!

There is no denying that this can happen even to seasoned traders but you can often prevent this disaster if you consider the other two trends first. Despite your daily uptrend, where was the DOW? Was it in phase 4 with a tendency to decline? When the DOW collapses, most stocks follow. How about the weekly? Although the daily showed an uptrend, the weekly may well have been at resistance or even in a downtrend and a quick check of that would have made you more cautious.

Its best, and safest approach is to follow the three trends in order. Having checked the phase of the broader market, look next at the weekly chart of any stock of interest. If the weekly 22 EMA is pointing up, you would look for a long entry signal to buy on the daily chart. In other words, you want strength in the weekly and short term weakness on the daily that gives you a chance to buy a stock at a bargain price. The exact opposite is true for shorting. If the weekly is down trending (as per the 22 EMA), look for shorting opportunities on the daily chart.

You are making strategic decisions at the weekly level. In other words the weekly chart tells you if you should go long or short by its trend direction. You then make tactical decisions (if you are going to enter and at what price) on the daily price chart.

The Third Little Secret: Select the Appropriate Trading Strategy

There are three strategies that I use. The first is the conventional "going long" or buying a stock in the belief that it will be at a higher price in the next 5 or so days when I will sell. The second is the exact opposite strategy, "going short". Here we see that a stock is likely to drop in price over the next week and we sell it, with the expectation that we will be able to buy it back "buy to cover", at a lower price soon. The third trading strategy is to use covered calls.

You will be making most of these decisions at the individual stock level. It not uncommon for an individual stock to move in the opposite direction to the broader market. But what we are trying to do here is to improve our chances of making money above the simple 50:50 chance we would expect from pure luck.

Your chances of a stock moving with the market are much greater than of it moving against, so do what the market tells you—unless your indicators give you a very strong signal which we will look at later.

If the Dow is trending up, you would be looking for stocks that are trending up on the weekly chart. This is an opportunity to go long **when the daily chart of that stock is showing weakness** and you can buy it at a bargain price with a good chance of rallying in a few days to make you some money! Don't worry about how to determine if there is a good chance of a rally yet—we will look at indicators later that will tell you these things. At this stage we are just deciding what our strategy will be. If the Dow is in phase one or two, you also have the opportunity to look for stocks to buy and sell covered calls against. More detail on that strategy in a separate section.

If the Dow is in phase three (the top of the hill), you can still go long with cautious stops in place and you can also look to go short with similar caution. At this phase, covered calls are no longer a good idea because when the next phase comes along and stocks drop, you will be left with a much depreciated stock that can take years to recover to its purchase price . . . . if ever!

If the Dow is in phase 4 (the downhill run) your only sensible alternative is to sell short. You would be looking for stocks that have a downtrending weekly chart.

Then you would want to find temporary strength in the daily chart, sell short and buy to cover in a few days or a weeks' time when the price has dropped. This is definitely NOT the time for covered calls.

The Fourth Little Secret: Stick to the rules

There are a lot of rules which we will develop during the rest of the book. There are rules for stock selection. There are rules for entering and exiting a stock. There are massively important rules about stop losses, and there are rules about money management.

The biggest failing of all novice traders is an inability to stick to the rules. I know you think you are different, but you are not! I know that because I think I am different but even after 6 years of professional trading, I still find myself breaking the rules sometimes. I'm especially prone to rule breaking when I have had a run of wins and I start to think that I can beat "the market".

Every single time you break the rules, you will get smashed! You cannot beat the market. People smarter than all of us are out there making a living from taking our money. The only way you can make money from the stock market is to have a well-defined set of rules and to absolutely stick to them.

I used to ask (rhetorically) in my trading classes: "who has tried to quit smoking and can't? Who has tried to lose weight and failed? Who has begun a degree and dropped out?". These people are very unlikely to be successful traders. Trading is about discipline and discipline is the ability to stick to the rules.

What Stocks to Trade

This question preoccupies people to such an extent that many other people have made a lot of money selling stock selection programs! Of course you don't need these because they don't work.

There are plenty of ways you can select your own stocks. You can run screens on most charting programs or indeed your trading platform, to find stocks which are making new highs or lows, trending up or down or forming some sort of pattern.

The fact is, it doesn't really matter what stocks you use— as long as they exhibit consistent patterns that you can trade!

There are several ways to select stocks to trade. The first is to generate a "watchlist" of 10 to 20 stocks that you have heard off, someone has mentioned, or you have read about. They should have reasonable daily average volume (say over 500,000 a day) so that you can get in and out of them easily ie they are "liquid". They should also have a consistent pattern of movement with which you become very familiar.

A good way to start a watchlist is with stocks you know already or in which you have an interest. If you like motor bikes try Harley Davidson (HOG). If you like retail how about Walmart (WMT). If you like white goods how about Whirlpool (WHR) and so on. Think of an industry segment and look up that segment on your trading platform or Yahoo finance or CNBC. Have a look at a few stocks in a sector of interest. Find one that seems to move in predictable ways, one that you like.

A second way is to use a filter which can be easily done in any trading or charting program. There are usually preset filters and you can use these to begin with. Look for charts with an up trending channel for example. Refine the search with more specific parameters like volume (greater than 500,000) price (below $50 is a good start) and other parameters. Once you have narrowed the universe of stocks down to a list of 50 or less, have a look at them and see if they fit your idea of a stock that is going up! You can refine the search criteria as often as you like.

Another way to select stocks (and I include ETF's as well) is to find someone else doing a good job and piggyback on them! You can use a group of professional traders like those at a site called spiketrade.com. Any decent site like this will cost you money and this one is about $90 per month. However you don't actually need to join. All you want are some stock ideas. Those that have worked in the past are as good as those that are working now and you can access this sites historical data for free as a guest. You only need a few good stocks that you learn inside out.

Whichever way you select stocks doesn't matter—it will probably be a combination of methods. No matter how you end up with a list of stocks to trade, how do you find the one or two trades you want to trade this week? The idea is to trade well, not to trade often so one trade a week is OK. If there are no good trades in any week, it's a perfectly valid strategy to stand down and do nothing. If you are overwhelmed with brilliant opportunities to trade, take two, three or even up to six in a week. In my opinion that's as many as anyone can manage properly.

Technical Analysis

The charting program that I use Incredible Charts, has over 100 technical indicators to choose from. Others have even more. Each of these has numerous parameters which can be changed as well, making up many thousands of possible ways to analyse a stock. In my world of simplification I think you need only four.

It is helpful to review why we use technical analysis. We are looking for patterns in a stocks price movement which occur regularly. If we can predict the occurrence of a pattern with some accuracy, we can buy low and sell high (or the opposite for shorting) and take a profit in the process. We need to find some indicators that can help us do that.

The things that matter in this case are the opening price, the closing price and the high and low set during the day (OHLC). As well, we want to know how the OHLC prices of today, compare with previous days, weeks and months. In other words we need to know if the price range is wide or narrow compared to the past and the amount of interest in the stock (shown by volume). We also need to know if the price is trending and if it is at the beginning, middle or end of a trend.

If we know all these things, we are in a position to make an educated guess about whether the current price is likely to continue up, down or sideways and how we can profit from that expected movement.

The Four Indicators

For any particular stock, I have four indicators that I use. As already mentioned I use www.incrediblecharts. com to do all my charting. I am very familiar with it and it allows me to draw all the lines I need. It covers Australian stocks as well as US and most others. It also has all indices, and a great search function. The cost is about A$20 per month but there are loads of others and there are pretty good free ones too like bigcharts.com. Find one that can do everything you want and get really familiar with it. This tool will make you money—learn to use it well.

If you want to know the hows and whys of particular indicators, you will have to look them up! I don't really care how or why they work anymore than I care how my computer works. I just care **that** they work.

Most programs come with pre-set parameters and most people don't change them. This means if you use preset parameters you are looking at things the same way as most other people. Since we are looking at crowd behavior and trying to predict it, this is a good thing! Leave the parameters as they are in most cases.

Charts are messy and can be confusing and we are about to make them a little messier—or so it will seem in the beginning. The mess will start to mean something before too long and as you might expect, we will add as little as possible.

The First Indicator

The Traders Action Zone (TAZ) is identified by a pair of exponential moving averages.

Add a 22 period EMA and a 13 period EMA. I use the term period in a generic sense, it will be daily on a daily chart and weekly on a weekly chart. The longer term EMA (the 22 period) tells you if you are in an uptrend—if pointing up, or a downtrend if pointing down. The area between the two moving averages forms what I call the Taz—the Traders Action Zone. Others refer to this as the value zone. When the price of the stock is in the Taz, it is at fair value.

It's the same as when you are shopping for groceries. You might like King Island triple bree (I do) but its too expensive to buy usually. You know what the usual price is so that when you see it on special you know it's a value buy and you buy heaps! It's the same with stocks. The Taz identifies for you when the stock is on sale. Buy it when its good value.

In an uptrend, price tends to move from the Taz to the upside and then return to the Taz. In a downtrend, it moves from the Taz to an area below it before moving back to the Taz. Have a look at any chart you like and you will see this pattern repeating itself.

Wait . . . . a pattern! That's exactly what we are looking for. You will see it on both the weekly and the daily charts. Immediately we have something we can trade. Clearly you buy when the price is in the Taz and you sell . . . . when? The next indicator helps with that decision.

The Second Indicator:—channels

Add a channel to either of the EMA's. I say either because some will work with a channel on the 13 day (or week) and others work better with the 22 period. It doesn't matter and you can change them all the time. This is not science—its art. You want to find a channel that contains about 95% (in other words most) of the highs and lows of the price pattern over the last two months. Charting programs allow you to do this by adjusting the percentage width of the band. Again play with this because it will almost certainly be different for each stock.

As an example I usually start with the 13 period EMA because I am trying to find the range of prices for a shorter period of time rather than longer. Most stocks seem to fall within a 4% to 8% range on the daily chart, wider on the weekly. Just keep clicking until you end up with a channel that contains most of the price action for that stock.

The channel is the range of movement of price for that stock. The Taz is the area of value. Uptrending stocks should be purchased in or below the Taz. Sometimes there is some bad news and the stock will move below that area toward the bottom of the channel. Perfect— buy it there. Use either the Taz (if bought below) as the target price or the upper channel, if you purchased in the Taz. Ofcourse the opposite is true if you are shorting.

Always look backwards (to the left of the chart) for support or resistance. These areas have a habit of repeating themselves. Try and buy at an area of support and sell or set price targets at an area where the price has stalled in the past ie at resistance.

You will note that at areas of both support and resistance another common pattern often occurs. In the case of a stock that is about to turn up, it will tend to open low, spike down and often break through an area of support, and then finish well above the lows of the day. This sort of price movement puts in what is known as a hanging man (at bottoms) in candlestick parlance or a gravestone doji at tops.

Dr Elder calls them Kangaroo tails which is a term that means more to me than the candlestick stuff. Anyway they look like this:

The first Kangaroo Tail at the high on the 19th of September 2013, is perfect. Others at tops and bottoms are marked. Like all indicators, these are not absolute. Changes in price direction occur without Kangaroos tails forming or with only small tails as can be seen on many occasions on this chart. Also Tails can form without a change in direction following and there are plenty of examples of that on the chart as well.

If you see a stock that has formed a Kangaroo Tail AND the other indicators also suggest a change in direction, then its time to put your money on the table.

Now we have the Taz and channels to guide our decisions, (combined with Kangaroo Tails). Two more indicators to make up the four I use.

The third indicator:—the Moving Average Convergence Divergence (MACD) histogram

Again I don't change the settings from the default. The MACD histogram is a bar chart which measures the difference between a short term moving average and a longer term MA.

When the pattern it makes is moving up, the short term trend is bullish—short term prices are rising faster than the longer term so there is a gold rush going on. When its moving in the downward direction, the short term trend is bearish—the trend is likely to continue down.

You can think of the pattern as a rubber band stretching both above the zero line and below. At full stretch in either direction, the most likely next move is back towards the centre. You can use history to see how far the rubber band usually stretches for any particular stock.

When the pattern is heading upwards, especially on a turn from the bar that looks like it represents "full stretch", another part of the buy signal is formed for a long position. The reverse is just as true for shorting. You can use the opposite turn to also assist with determining when to exit.

Remember that you need to combine all indicators to have the best picture. The MACD—H on its own can be misleading—as is true for every indicator. Combine it with the other 3 here and you have a much better chance of getting a correct entry or exit signal.

The fourth indicator:—the Stochastic

The stochastic belongs to the group of indicators known as oscillators which are the nearest thing possible to a genuine predictor of market movements or leading indicator. I use an exponential indicator to smooth out the bumps and I use the preset parameters. The stochastic moves between two reference lines—usually at 80% and 20%. When the indicator gets below 20% the stock is considered "oversold" meaning its due to rally. When price is over the 80% mark, its called "overbought" which means it is likely to sink soon.

Be aware that because of its "leading" nature, the stochastic can give premature signals. I have seen it referred to (unkindly) as a "mis-leading" indicator! I use it a lot in combination with the others as outlined below to identify trading opportunities. I also use its movement into the oversold or overbought range as an exit strategy. Many times this will give you an early signal and you could have made more money if you'd stayed in . . . sure you would have! I would rather be out early having made a small profit than stay in the trade and watch a profit turn to a loss.

Here is a daily chart of Owens Corning (OC) showing all the indicators I use:

Notice how I have drawn the channels on the 13 day EMA to encompass most of the price action. It's very easy to trade in hindsight so take a piece of paper and cover all the bars to the right of the arrows I have drawn in September 2013.

At that arrow, a Kangaroo Tail has formed right at the upper channel. The MACD-H is at full stretch above the line and the stochastic is overbought (above the 80% line). There is a good probability that this stock price will decline.

Now move the paper and note that ofcourse it did decline (otherwise I wouldn't have used this example!). It dropped right through to the bottom of the channel. What a great stock to short (or buy a Put) the day after you saw that Kangaroo Tail form. The same situation occurs for entering a long position, around the 12th of November.

Note that this stock moves from one side of the channel to the other but hangs around the Taz on the way. If you are nervous or more short term (as I am) you would probably exit when the price enters the Taz. You sacrifice potential profit, but you avoid the risk of the stock moving back from the Taz to the same side of the channel as it did in December.

Now you have enough indicators to find good stocks to trade for a consistent profit. You may find others, but be wary of trying too many. Learn these first and start to make money before you try other indicators. Then as you do try new things, make sure that you are tracking the results so that you can see if you are really getting better or not.

Enough theory lets get into this business of making money. Start with the weekly chart—where one bar equals a week. You get a better perspective on the longer term trend this way. Look at about two years. The weekly is where you make strategic decisions—is this a stock to go long, short or leave alone?

Earlier I let you into the four secrets of making money in stocks. The fourth secret is to stick to the rules and here are three important ones relating to stock selection. These rules cost me a fortune to develop, please do not ignore them unless you also want to lose a fortune re-inventing them!

RULE 1. ***Never short a stock that has an uptrending weekly chart. Conversely never buy a stock (go long) when its chart is downtrending***

Stocks which have a clear trend usually have stronger movements in the direction of the trend than against it. If you are quick and lucky you might be able to pick a short term move in the opposite direction to the trend. If you are wrong, or too slow and you find yourself on the wrong side of a move, you will get stopped out and lose money. Why take the risk?

There is ONE exception to rule one and that is if there is a divergence between the MACD histogram and the price chart. This is a Dr Elder special and a real beauty which I will cover later.

If you can't work out if a weekly chart is uptrending, downtrending or just drifting sideways, find the nearest five year old and ask them! That's how simple it is. You are just looking for a pattern. Ensure that the chart is showing at least two years of data and look to see if the chart is sloping upwards from bottom left to top right. Yes? Then you are in an uptrend. If it slopes downward from top left to bottom right, you have a downtrend. It may be drifting along between two reasonably well defined lines and you can trade that too (although a little differently). Kids are brilliant at seeing these patterns. If neither you nor your five year old assistant can see the pattern, then its probably not there so move on.

Dennis Wall

Lets say you have found a stock with an uptrending weekly chart. According to rule 1, you can start to think about going long in this stock. Only start thinking! There are other technical parameters to consider first.

Once the weekly chart tells you that there is a chance to enter, you flick to the Daily chart. If the daily chart is in agreement with the weekly, then you may look at the tactical decisions of when to enter and exit and where to place your stop loss. Here is a good place for the second rule:

RULE 2: *only enter a position when the weekly and daily charts are in agreement*

You will often find a brilliant weekly chart screaming that this is the time to enter say a long position. A kangaroo tail has formed at the Taz of an uptrending chart, the MACD-H is at full stretch below the zero line and the Stochastic is below the 20% line and turning up. Then you turn to the daily chart full of expectation . . . . and find all the indicators tell you the exact opposite! Waste no more time, just move on to the next stock. We are trying to maximize the chance of a stock moving in our favour. There is a greater chance of this happening if the weekly and the daily price charts are in agreement.

RULE 3: *avoid trading companies that will be reporting earnings within the next two weeks*

Using your brokers site, Finviz.com, yahoofinance, earningswhispers.com or somewhere similar, check to see if the stock is going to report earnings within the time frame of your trade ie within the next week or two. If so avoid this stock until the reporting is over.

Usually when a company reports earnings that are better than expectations, the stock value jumps. Conversely, when a company "misses" earnings, the stock drops. However, there a plenty of examples of the exact opposite happening. Some people believe they are smart enough to predict these events and the subsequent stock movement and try and trade them. I am not one of those people. The response to earnings is usually unpredictable and often violent. The best thing you can do is avoid stocks that will be reporting earnings within your trading timeframe.

Money Management

If there is one key to making money from stocks it is not stock selection, use of indicators, amount of capital or anything else. The secret to making money from the stock market is managing your money.

Money management refers to the rules you put in place to protect and grow your capital. As a trader your first job is to protect your capital. Your second task is to grow that capital. The way to achieve both is through money management. I use a modified version of the oft quoted 2% and 6% rules. The 2% rule says that you cannot risk more than 2% of your capital in any one trade. It is this rule that determines the size of any position that you take.

Lets say you have $100,000. The 2% rule says you may not risk more than $2,000 on any one trade. If you find a $20 stock and there is a natural stop at say $18 (we will look at protective stops or stop losses later) then there is a $2 risk in that trade. You may only buy $2,000/ $2 = 1,000 stocks. I said I modified that a bit and I do that by deciding how much of a dollar loss I am prepared to take. I might feel more comfortable if the most I can lose on a trade is $1,000. In that case, I can only buy $1,000/$2 = 500 shares.

You can always reduce the 2% rule but you may never increase it—that is, if you want to survive as a trader.

The 6% rule says that you can never risk more than 6% of your total capital at any time. If you have three positions with 2% risk then you cannot enter any more positions until one or more of the existing trades is closed. If you have less risk per trade then you can open more positions.

Alex Elder recommends that if you ever hit that 6% loss, you stop trading for the month and just paper trade. If you take a 6% loss in your portfolio there is something wrong and you need to take a break, analyse your trades and yourself before you step back in. Losing streaks do happen and you need to take a breather and find out why. Sometimes the market has changed without you picking it up or you are just off your game. I have not had to exercise this part of the 6% rule for years but when I did, it really enabled me to get back on track.

Record Keeping

You can read every book there is on trading, attend every seminar and paper trade till you are blue in the face—I guarantee that you will still make mistakes in your trading! Correct money management will prevent these mistakes from threatening your capital so just accept that mistakes are part of your trading life. Mistakes are not a problem—but you must learn from them so as not to keep making the same mistakes. Keeping good records and anlaysing what went wrong as well as what went right with each and every trade is the answer.

I went to a trading seminar recently and the presenter made the case for record keeping as the means by which you can become your own teacher. He is dead right. You must record everything you do. In the text box on the next page are the columns I use in my spreadsheet to capture the data on every trade I undertake. I use this to sort and analyse my trades every month, quarter and year to see how many winners I had, how many losers, what grade they were, how much I made and every other aspect of the trades.

I even analyse what day of the week I enter and exit. Although I don't physically add a chart anymore, when I am reviewing I go back to the chart and look at my entry and exit points. Its much easier to see what you did right or wrong when you have a few more bars to see what happened after you made your call.

Column Headings for Recording Trades

Entry Date, Long/short, Symbol, Position Size, Entry Price, Stop Loss, Target Price, Exit Date, Exit Price, Profit/Loss, Days in Trade, Grade (see below).

What you are trying to achieve here is to constantly increase the value of your portfolio, or in other words to have a constantly increasing equity curve on a monthly basis. Record the total value of your portfolio (from your brokers' statement) every month and plot it. Aim for a nice even uptrend. Review every trade at the end of each month and see what went right and what went wrong. Where are the strengths and weaknesses in your trading?

Until recently I kept a paper trading diary rather than an electronic one because I liked to be able to flick through the charts and scribble on them. I faithfully printed the charts for every trade and pasted them onto the left page of a scrap book. I had the weekly and daily charts for entry and the daily chart only for the exit.

On the right page I recorded all the details of the trade. You can do either paper or electronic (although the scrap book takes a lot of time and is environmentally unfriendly). But be sure to keep detailed records which you review regularly. I believe this simple practice has done more to improve my trading than any other single thing and I believe good records will improve yours as well.

I mentioned grading your trades. This is another tip I picked up from Alex Elder. You take the dollar amount per share that you made between buying and selling a stock and you divide that by the dollar width of the channel.

If you took 0-10% of the channel then you earn a "D" grade. 10% to 20% is a "C". If you take 20% to 30% of the channel width in profit then you are a "B" and above that is an "A".

Your aim is to be a consistent A Grade trader. Don't be discouraged—its harder than you think to take 30% or more of the channel.

Finding a trade

Now we have a watchlist, the four indicators set up, our record keeping designed and money management rules in place. Lets go through the actual process of finding and entering a trade as well as setting the three prices every trade must have—entry, protective stop and target.

I have a list of about 20 stocks I call my "C list". These are the tools of my trade so I really learn them. You need to watch how their price responds to news, earnings and geopolitical events. Do they move in line with an index or are they independent? I love to have something like SLV (a silver ETF) on my list because precious metals tend to move in the opposite direction to the general market—not always though! I also use SLV as my main covered call position which I will describe later.

At weekends I first check the direction of the DOW or S&P500. If its upwards I have a bias towards going long. This is just a bias nothing more. Some stocks will perform in the opposite direction to the general market but as stated earlier, a rising tide tends to float all boats. Naturally if the market is down, then I have a bias towards going short.

I also look at the VIX (the volatility index) which usually moves in the opposite direction to the DOW. You can think of it as the "fear index". When the VIX is low it means there is little fear in the market and stocks tend to move upwards. If the VIX is high, there is a lot of fear out there and the market tends to move lower.

Finally I look at the exchange rate to see if it's a good time to keep my money in the US or if I would make money just by bringing it back into Singapore today! I don't play the forex game itself but you can follow the USD /SGD or USD/AUD index in your charting program in the same way as a stock. When it's very high you can bring some cash back to your own currency and wait for it to turn before sending it back if you wish.

Then I run through my "C List" with my chart program set on weekly charts to see if there are any that are likely to be tradable in the next week. All stocks initially reside in the C list. If I find a weekly chart which is uptrending, then I look to the indicators to see if they support a trade on the long side. (The reverse is true for shorting).

Is the price at the TAZ, a line of support or the bottom of the channel? If so, is the MACD Histogram at full stretch below its central line and started to make a turn upwards?

Finally is the stochastic in the oversold area below the 20% line and turning up? Refer to the chart of OC on page 121 for a couple of good examples of this situation in mid-October and mid-November 2013 on a daily chart. Its looks the same on a weekly.

If all these conditions are not met, we just flick on down to the next weekly chart. We are looking for reasons NOT to trade at this stage. If ALL these conditions are met, we MAY have a stock that can be traded from the long side. In that case move to the daily chart of the stock and check exactly the same things. Don't forget rule 1 above (don't trade against the trend).

Is a stock meets rule 2 (your assessment of the weekly and daily charts agree) then save that chart to either you're "A list" or "B list". Sometimes you find yourself with a stock that is obvious you need to enter on Monday. Then move it to the A list, that's the "action now" list. Sometimes it looks as if the stock **might** be right to trade but you really need another bar or two to confirm, then it goes into the B list.

On Monday enter positions for the stocks on the A list. Each day review the B list to see if you get a strong entry signal with a bit more information. Forget the C list till next weekend. This way you only have 5 or 6 stocks to review on a daily basis and the search for entries doesn't become overwhelming.

By the way, in order to be able to enjoy my weekends without fear that the market is going to move against me, I try to be flat (no open trades) before the weekend. This is not a golden rule but it's a good idea. By Wednesday I would usually have my 6 positions open and the rest of the week my focus is on exiting those at maximum profit. The same applies if you are travelling, tired, or otherwise unable to focus. Exit your open positions and stand back for a while.

Don't worry if some weeks you're A list is bare! You are under no obligation to take a trade. If you don't find a perfect set of charts just stay in cash. Don't trade just because you feel you should. Trading is a dangerous business with unseen risks lurking everywhere. Unless you get pretty close to perfect direction from the charts, stay out!

When to trade

Lots of people who are not resident in the US whine about the inconvenient times that the US market is open. Whine away—neither the NYSE nor the other 14 trading floors in the US are going to change their hours for you! Figure out when is the best time for you to trade and then stick to those times.

In Singapore, the market opens at 9:30 pm during the US summer and 10:30 pm during the US winter. I do my analysis in the morning because I am most alert then. Then I go to the gym and spend the rest of the day with the family. After dinner I go for a run, shower and shave and get ready to trade the first two hours of the market.

Forget what everyone says about "amateur hour" being the first hour and the pros trading the last hour. Some commentators go to great lengths to analyse the general price trends at different *times* of the day! Traders supposedly all go to lunch together between 12 and 2pm so prices are supposed to drift downwards then on lower volume. Morning and afternoon tea times have different effects on prices. If this were true, there would be millions of millionaire day traders . . . . and there are not!

If you have done your homework correctly, you know at what price you will enter and exit a trade. Who cares when those prices are hit? I have found that if I sit up all night, I am still no better off than if I just enter my orders and go to bed.

We are not day trading here. Swing traders really only need end of day prices to make decisions. You get the end of day price the next day, in our time frames. You have all day to decide what you want to do. Decide what times you are able to trade most effectively and then forget stocks for the rest of the day.

It might be impractical for you to be up at the start of the trading day if its say 12:30am or 1:30 am in Australia. But there is nothing stopping you getting up at

5 or 6 am and trading the last hour or two of the market. If that's too hard . . . . well no-one is forcing you to trade. A genuine alternative is to trade the market that operates where you live—Australia.

The same selection criteria apply to the Australian market but be careful of liquidity. The entire ASX 200 trades about 600 million shares daily compared with the US S&P 500 which trades nearly 4 **billion** per day. That means that you can sometimes have trouble finding a buyer or seller when you want to trade in Australia. You can minimize this problem by electing to trade only stocks with big volumes.

Setting the Entry, Target and a Protective Stop

Once you've decided to take a trade, you need to determine in advance the three prices that every trade must have: Entry, Target and Protective Stop (otherwise known as Stop Loss). These parameters simply must be set in the cool hard light of (your) day when your mind is clear and there is no pressure from the market being open. They will determine the size of the trade, your risk and even if you will still take the trade.

Entry is discussed in more detail below but for the purpose of designing your trade, lets use yesterdays close as the entry price. Assume that the stock finished at $25 yesterday, your entry point will be if the stock opens at $25. Now you need to determine the protective stop.

You probably selected this stock because it put in a kangaroo tail near the Taz or the bottom of the channel. Most people will now select the bottom of the tail as the stop loss. That's a good spot but better, is to then put a round number between your stop and the market. The market has a weird habit of hovering around round numbers because this is where most people put their stops! So if the Kangaroo tail went down to $24.50, put your stop at $24.49.

That gives you a $25 - $24.49 = .51 loss if you get "stopped out". If 2% of your portfolio value is $2000 then you can buy 2,000 / .51 = 3,921 stocks. Now you have set your Protective stop level and your trade size.

Now look at the nearest likely high that this stock can make. You will tend to be over-optimistic about this one so be as realistic as possible. Likely targets are the Taz, the upper limit of the envelope (channel) or a recent line of support or resistance. Before you enter the trade, the higher the target, the more excited you become. You are already deciding what to spend the profits on!

Once you are in the trade, the fear of a profit turning into an overnight loss is often so great that you will not get anywhere near to that far away number before you press the sell button. So choose a level that is genuinely achievable judging by recent performance of the stock, and be brave about sticking to it. This may end up being where you exit or you may choose to use the trailing stop method discussed below but you need to set the target before you enter the trade.

Its very easy to put all this data into a simple spreadsheet which will calculate it all for you. I include a column which shows the win:loss ratio. If the target is not at least three times the size of the stop loss, don't enter the trade. If you use a 3:1 profit vs loss ratio and you practice rigid money management techniques, you are almost (**almost**) assured of success. If I end up with several trades but the 6% rule says that I can't take them all, then I use the ratio to determine the best trades (highest ratio) and enter those.

You may also want to look at the time it has taken for the stock to move between your anticipated purchase price and target in the past. This can give you an idea of your time target as well. This is not one that I am to fussed about since I mainly enter early in any week and try to be out by the end of the week, but it can give you an idea of how long you may have to hold this stock and therefore when you will have enough capital to trade again.

Once you have entered this stock you will have put a maximum of 2% of your capital at risk. That means you can only enter three more positions to remain within the 6% rule. If you drop the 2% to 1% then you can enter six positions in total.

Having set all these parameter you are ready to actually trade:

Executing an Entry and Exit

There are many thoughts about how to enter a position. One is that you wait for a confirmation that your assessment is correct by waiting for the price to break the previous days close. You determine to enter when the price is one cent above that limit. The problem with this is that unless the stock keeps on climbing like crazy, you often end up buying at a higher price than you could have. On the plus side you have confirmed that a rally is indeed underway. This is a totally acceptable way to choose an entry and with correct use of stops and targets, will still end up with a good profit.

Another way if you have the interest and the patience, which will usually give you a better entry, is to use the 1, 2 or 5 minute chart to determine your entry. Prices perform in exactly the same way on these short term charts as they do on daily or weekly charts. Prices will rally, then fall back to the Taz. Instead of just buying the first time the price rallies past the previous days high, you can use that event as your trigger to confirm that you are going to enter this trade, then wait for a pullback to actually make the purchase. This method is a little more stressful and you must be sure that you don't end up chasing a stock and getting a worse price, but with practice will often yield better results.

Most important is not to chase a stock. Once you have decided on a price that you think is reasonable, enter that price in your system and go to bed. If you get filled then great, if you don't, then no problem. You can always try another entry next night or find another stock.

Trading stocks is like trading anything else, you make your money by purchasing a bargain. Chasing a runaway stock price often ends in you paying too much for there to be any profit left in the short rally we are chasing.

Having entered a position, you must then enter your pre-determined protective stop. I wait a while to be sure that the stock is not going to whip down and take me out before making a massive rally! But you must enter it that trading day—before you go to bed. If the price does dip down and triggers your stop—that's life. The stop is there to protect your capital. Often you will get whipsawed out as they say, usually because in your caution, you are setting the stop too close to the entry price.

When a stock dips down—seemingly with malice—trips your stop then rallies like crazy, it hurts! Don't let it. There is no point getting upset over this, it happens to professionals and beginners alike. Don't look back to beat yourself up. By all means look back to see if you can learn something about setting stops for the future but if a stop is hit then your strategy is working and your capital is only reduced by a small amount.

Sometimes the market will simply act in a totally unpredictable manner and the stock you have so carefully analysed just does the opposite thing. When that happens be thankful you put your stop in place. You could have lost a lot more!

On occasions, a stock will gap down through your stop which means that it opens below your sell price so the protective sell order is not triggered. There is nothing you can do about that either. Just accept that the stop has been broken, you are going to lose money but you now use your knowledge of technical analysis and the 5 minute chart to try and get out at the best price possible. Even when a stock is tanking, there will be moments when the price retraces near the Taz. Wait for those moments to occur then get out. You lose money but you live to fight another day. If you lose more than 6% of your capital, tighten up your stops on remaining positions, exit them all as soon as possible and then sit the game out for a month. Use the time to paper trade and review previous trades for what went right and what went wrong.

Some people use bracket orders to enter both their protective stop and target price in the one order. I have this nagging feeling that I am signaling too much of my intentions to the opposition if I do this, but then again maybe I am just paranoid. I do use bracket orders if I am travelling and may not have access to high speed internet at the right time of day. Your two important prices (target and stop) are set and will be automatically activated in your absence so you can pretty much relax.

Managing the Trade

Now you are in a trade and the stop (and possibly the target) is in position. Each day you wake up and check the charts excitedly. If the stock has not triggered your stop loss, then you have a choice, to leave the stop where it is or to move it up. If the price has not made a new low that day, move the stop up. Move it to just below the lowest price of the preceeding day every day that a higher low is put in. Keep moving up as fast as possible to your purchase price. It is the nicest of feelings when you get to this stage because you can no longer lose money! You are now just playing with other people's money. Yours is nice and safe, locked in with a stop loss at or above the purchase price.

From here on, you are worrying about how much you will make rather than how much you can lose. You have your price target in mind or entered as a bracket order but will the stock get there before the weekend? What if someone starts a war or something over the weekend? When should you really get out?

One answer to this conundrum is to use a trailing stop as the price nears your target or at least moves up and away from your purchase price. A trailing stop allows you to set how much of a retracement you will allow that day before the stock is automatically sold for you. Lets say you look at the 5 minute chart and you see the stock moving up with a range of twenty cents per bar. You can set the trailing stop so that a sell order will be triggered if the price moves backwards by twenty cents. As the price moves up, your stop keeps moving up to twenty cents below the latest high. This method can help to maximize profit but as with all stops, be careful not to trail too close so that you get whipsawed out of a nice rally.

The only other thing you need to worry about is if the progress of the rally slows too far away from your target. In other words you feel like you are running out of time to reach the target. If in doubt, get out! Its much better to take an early profit and miss your target than to watch a profit turn to a loss while you wait for the target.

Obviously if the price looks like it will power through your target, take the bracket order out and let the price run up to your next target. However, if things are taking too long, gravity might be getting a grip of your stock and it can act pretty fast! Take a gift when offered—you can always re-enter if the indicators are right.

And there you have it—how to enter, protect and exit a stock. Once you have entered a position, record it as shown in the section on record keeping. Remember you keep these records not just to fill in your time, but to learn from every trade. Analyse the records weekly and monthly. Even though I keep electronic daily records, I print out the list of trades at the end of the month, paste it into a scrapbook and then write a page or so about what I did right, wrong and could do to improve.

The final measurement is to record your portfolio value at the end of every month—your stock broker program will do this for you. Graph the figure and check that you are getting a nice smooth upwards curve. There will be months where things go backwards a little but they should be few and far between. Once continuous growth is achieved over a period of 6 months or more, you are well on the way to being a professional trader!

Options and Covered Calls

I mentioned at the beginning of this chapter that I once spent a lot of time writing Covered Calls. They are not my favourite anymore for one reason—they cost me over $1million US! Now I use a simplified version only when the market is in stage 2—that nice strong uptrend.

Covered calls involves selling Call options once you already own the underlying stock. There are two types of options, Puts and Calls. We will just focus initially on Calls. There is a good way to use Puts if you can't short a stock and we will look at Puts later.

Options exist in property too and stock options are similar. When you want to buy a house, you sign an "option to purchase". This is a document that says you are going to pay the vendor an agreed amount for the house in a month or maybe two. When you sign an option to purchase, you pay an amount (usually 1% of the agreed purchase price) to prove your intention to purchase. If you don't eventually go ahead with the purchase, you lose that amount.

In the stock market just as the property market, the "option to purchase" is simply known as an "option". The amount you have to pay when you sign your "option to purchase" is called the "premium" in the world of the stock market, the value of which is determined by the market.

So if you wanted to buy a stock in a months' time at a certain price, you could buy a Call option just by paying the premium. But where does this option come from? It is made out of thin air by the person who owns the original stock—that's you. The technical term for made out of thin air is "written". You write calls to sell them to someone else.

I used to have a long and complex list of criteria for selecting stocks for writing covered calls. Now I use SLV (a silver ETF). I use this because I like commodities like gold and silver long term. Consequently if I ever am left holding this ETF at a price lower than I paid, I don't worry. I know it will always rally. Naturally I still try to buy at a bargain and when I think it will rally over the course of a week or so.

I also like SLV because you can sell calls that mature in a week. Most stocks (not all) only have calls that mature in a month. A month is way too long for my time horizon. Here's how it works:

Let's say SLV is trading at $20 and using your usual indicators, you think it is likely to rally a bit over the next week. You buy at $20. You then sell a $20 Call a week out for say $0.25. That's a 1.2% return in a week—pretty good. The best thing about this is that you get that 1.2% return no matter what happens to the stock price. Sounds fantastic doesn't it—and it is.

If the stock finishes at $20, you get "called". In other words your stock is sold automatically at the same price you paid for it. And you still keep the 25 cents per share you got a week ago for selling the call. You are now back in cash, ready to go again.

If the stock finishes the week at less than $20, you get to keep the stock. And you still keep the 25 cents per share you got a week ago! If this happens, you just keep on selling $20 calls each week until you get called. You may not get 25 cents if the price of the ETF has dropped a fair way. If you can get **anything** for selling a $20 call, just do it. If you can't get any premium, then just wait till you can.

That's all I want to say about covered calls. If you want to read more then I recommend "Covered Calls and LEAPS a wealth option" by Hooper and Zalewski. Its hugely expensive (over $150) however it is the best book around on the topic and if you want to learn more, that's the place.

The other options I mentioned above called Puts. These are a very dangerous game but can be so lucrative under certain circumstances that you need to look at them closely.

Many times when you want to sell a stock short, the broker will not be able to fill your order. This is because it's a bit more complicated for brokers to find shares to effectively "lend" to you. Once you have at least a years practice with real money under your belt, one way around this is to buy a Put when you think a stock is about to crash. You would only do this if the exception to rule 1 is met—there is divergence between the MACD histogram and the stock price (see below).

If this situation arises and you can't sell shares short, look at the PUTS column in the list of options chains.

Select those options which expire in two or three months—no closer! Find a strike price that is "at the money" which means the strike price is very close to the current stock price. These puts will have a delta of about .50. The delta is a so called "greek" in options speak and measures rate of change of the value of the option. A delta of .50 means that if the stock drops in value by $1, the Put will gain in value by 50 cents. This is fantastic if the stock does as you expect—in this case falls. However, if the stock goes a little bit the other way you start to **lose** huge amounts of money!

Having found the "at the money" Put, calculate how many you want to buy. Be very careful here because these things have a limited life and you can't use stop losses for protection. In other words there is unlimited loss potential with Puts.

Consequently, assess the amount you are prepared to lose. This should be (as you now know) a maximum of 2% of your available capital. That's how many Puts you would buy, but remember that options are sold in "contracts" based on 100 shares. If you calculate you can afford to lose an amount of $1,000 and the appropriate Puts are selling for 36 cents, then you will be buying 1,000/.36 = 2,777. Divide this number by 100 and round down to arrive at the number of contracts you will buy = 27 contracts.

You want the share price now to plummet! If it does not within a few days, swallow your pride and take the loss and exit. Every day you stay in a Put position, you are losing money because the time value of the put is declining. The aim is to exit as fast as possible. You can't run trailing stops or anything else so minimize your risk by minimizing the time that you are in the position.

I know this all sound complex and high risk . . . . and it is. However the amount of money you can make on a small outlay is amazing! Returns of 30 to 40% are common, but so are losses of 100% if you stay in until expiration. It really depends on your risk appetite and money management ability.

MACD-H Divergence

The Put strategy is based on the premise that a stock is likely to make a sharp move downwards. This is most likely if the chart (both weekly and daily) has hit resistance—a price level that it has previously been unable to break up through. The chances of a decline are further enhanced if this level of resistance combines with the top of a price band and an upward facing Kangaroo tail has formed.

The overriding indicator that a stock may quickly decline is if the MACD histogram is showing a bearish divergence with the price action.

This is another gem that I have adopted from Dr Elder and you should read his books for more exact details. In general, if the price trend has been upwards but the MACD histogram has made a high above the mid line, dropped down then come back up and made a lower high, you have bearish divergence. That means the price is heading up, but if you join the tops of the two recent peaks of the MACD-H, the slope of that line is down.

You need this on **either** the weekly or daily chart and as mentioned above you need all the other indicators to be supportive. This is the one and only exception to rule number 1 (only trade in the direction of the trend). It is a very powerful and accurate indicator but sometimes only lasts for a few bars.

It also works in the opposite direction. If a stock has been downtrending and you have bullish MACD-H divergence (combined with all other indicators) then there is a good possibility of that stock rallying strongly. Remember to have divergence, the indicator must have crossed the zero line between the formation of the two highs or lows.

The danger of this strategy is entering too early. If you don't wait for confirmation that the MACD-H has really turned, you can find yourself on the wrong side of a strong move continuing in the direction of the current trend. In that case, exit fast! Things are not going to get better, so take the loss now before it gets bigger.

Trading stocks is a business. Like all businesses, sometimes it seems daunting. Sometimes its depressing. Sometimes its elating, sometimes boring. Like all new ideas its very easy to find reasons that you can't or don't want to get involved. All I can tell you is that trading is the ultimate "smart" way to make money. It will allow you to have enough cash to do anything you want. You must find enough interest to at least start with the charting. Once you can get over that hurdle, the rest will come with time.

All other businesses I know of require raw materials, manufacturing, staff, premises, equipment, marketing, and so on. This business requires none of those things—just a computer and an internet connection. The returns are far, far higher than any traditional business can even dream of and you can conduct this business anywhere. I do quite a bit of my trading on the boat. This is truly making money from knowledge and nothing else!

The only downside of this business that I have found is that its lonely! You just have to learn to cope with that. Its you and your computer against the brightest and the best, every single night. When you win you have beaten some of the smartest people on this planet. Celebrate with yourself a little, then get back on with the job. The work is lonely but the results allow you to live the lifestyle you have designed.

So please try and put any thoughts that you are not interested or can't figure it out, behind you. Anyone—and I mean **anyone**—can do this. You must try this if you aspire to financial freedom.

PART THREE

PUTTING IT ALL TOGETHER

The Key

The subtitle of this book is "How to retire before you are thirty", however the principals can be applied to retiring (defined as stopping working for someone else) at any time. If you start early enough you can definitely be leaving employment before you are thirty. If you have lost a few of those early years to what I euphemistically call "life experiences" (as I did), then you may not be ready to take the plunge into your new Lifestyle until a little later.

It doesn't matter when you do it, this book is designed to give you the tools to stop working for someone else and enjoy the lifestyle that you design, whenever you feel like so doing.

Here is the overall plan in a nutshell. This is "The Key" to living the life you choose, free of financial constraints. Read this key and re-read it until you can picture in your mind how this will work for you. This is the most important section of the book so I'd suggest photocopying it and sticking it on your mirror.

THE KEY

Maximise debt while you are young to buy as many cash positive investment properties as possible. The year before you choose to "retire" start selling off properties to pay down the debt on the remaining. Use a redundancy package or other savings to trade for additional cash flow. Start living.

To expand on this a little more in a series of straight forward steps:

1. Design the life you want. And how much money you need each month to fund it.
2. Get a job you enjoy and become the very best.
3. Move up the corporate tree as fast as possible to the highest paid position available.
4. Once you have been employed for more than 6 months, start buying houses using as much debt as the banks will lend you. The trick here is that they must be cash positive. Aim for 20. You must start early with this strategy to build up equity in the early ones.
5. Learn to swing trade US and/or Australian equities.
6. When you have reached the time to leave work, sell as many properties as necessary so that those remaining provide you with the income you need to fund your lifestyle. You are already financially free.
7. Get a redundancy package. Use the funds to trade stocks to give you even further income unrelated to employment. If you can't manage a redundancy, you will need to do this trading from savings.

Getting made redundant

The world of conventional economics depends on continuous economic growth. The simple question posed by most first year economics students when they realize this is . . . "but what happens if there is no continuous growth"? Well we should have learnt that during the GFC, but it seems we didn't.

Since there is no model to replace the existing one, companies go on trying to improve their profits year on year. With population growth in developed countries slowing to near zero and even slowing in developing countries, growth through increased sales is not going to happen.

If sales aren't increasing, the only way to improve profits is to reduce costs. The major way to do that is to improve "efficiency" which is nothing more than another term for "sack people". People are the biggest cost faced by nearly every conventional (as against e-commerce) industry. Even if you are a shipping company or airline where your biggest cost is fuel, the next is people.

In developed countries there is a sense of guilt about sacking perfectly good staff so words such as "downsizing" were developed to replace "mass sackings". Redundancy is another such word and is associated with a "guilt payment" to the person being sacked. These can be substantial like 18 months or more of regular salary! If you want to take advantage of this system, its important to be perceived as a valuable employee and just as important to be earning the highest salary possible.

Here is how to be made redundant.

Work your way to the highest paid position possible in the company. This is not a long term goal, its short term.

I am thinking of six months for every step. Use every possible means to jump the queue and reign in that next level job. Pull in favours, lose at golf games, button hole the chairman and board members. Corporations revel in their promotion on merit programs and all that stuff but everyone knows this is absolute nonsense in truth, especially at the top. You get promoted because the boss thinks you can achieve his goals and make him look good.

Be visible (for the right reasons) and make a noise. Make this your only goal for the next 6 months and focus on it exclusively. This is important for the rest of your life so there is nothing else more critical. Just get there. Why so much focus on this point? Well there are three reasons.

The first is that the higher up you can get, the more ability you have to delegate. This is critical in reducing your work load giving you time to learn how to trade or to buy properties. Second, the more income you have, the more you can borrow to maximize your income later. Third, as you rise through the ranks, you get paid more. In the end (and you will give them a helping hand at the right time) someone above is going to see that you are costing much more than a younger buck who could also do the job! Bingo, you are made redundant and all the benefits of this windfall are directly related to your current salary. From an altruistic perspective, there are lots of young people out there who need (or think they need) a break. Get out of their way and get on with the life you have designed!

The "cost reduction" rationale can be used in your favour to get you up the ladder fast. Maybe it hasn't occurred to the boss yet that you could do the job of a much more senior person at a lower cost. Lower to them may still mean a lot more to you. Let the boss know that . . . Win, win. Except of course for the guy whose job you take but then if he has set his life plan up properly then its win, win, win!

It may be that with all the pushing in the world, you have reached your glass ceiling. If it really is not possible to move to a higher paid position quickly, accept the fact and move on quickly to step two.

Now step two may not seem very ethical to you. I assure you that it is and the reason can be attributed to a man named Cyril Northcote Parkinson who penned his very well known Parkinsons Law in 1955. This law states work expands to fill the time available. The law applies to all things including time and space. For example, I have never seen a shed, big or small, that is not filled to overflowing within a few months of completion! Garages, cupboards under the stairs and any other storage area all fall within the same universal principal. In fact the same applies to computer storage and email accounts as well!

With regard to work, have you ever noticed how every single job magically fills the time allocated to it? The relevance to us is this; take your job which fills your entire week, and find a way to do the same job (or even more) in just 20% of the time—one day a week.

Sound ridiculous? One of the wonderful time management courses I once attended, asked all of us aspiring managers to recall how much work we got done on the day before a holiday compared to a normal day. Think about it. You can achieve almost a weeks work in the *afternoon* of the day before you go on leave, because **you only do what is absolutely critical and you let nothing distract you**.

If you apply this concept to your work every week, you can logically get the entire weeks work done on Monday if you only do what is critical and you let nothing distract you. To achieve this, you must however know what is really required of you in your job. By this I do **not** mean what is in your job description! I mean: what is it that you and only you, can and must do, to achieve the expected results of your job.

Everything else can be delegated to others. It really helps to review your job (and your boss's expectations) against what you actually do for a couple of weeks. You will find that you do an incredible amount of things that could be done by others. As regional manager for a multinational company, there were myriad reports, customer visits, factory tours, conference calls, financial reviews and so on, for which I was responsible. Every single one of them was actually performed by someone else. My job was really only to see that all these tasks were completed and to be able to answer any question about any of them from New York at any time! Once I discovered that, I was able to perform my role in less than one day a week.

If you can, try doing what lawyers do and keep a diary of what you actually do each day, broken into 15 minute intervals. You will be absolutely amazed at how little of importance you really achieve in a day! Again in my case, the blackberry resulted in me checking my email almost every minute (at work and at home) or every time the thing vibrated, which was much more frequently than that. The vast majority of these emails added no value to my primary job—none. But they certainly prevented me from doing much else.

All this might be a little harder if you are involved in manual work but even then, the higher up the tree you climb, the more you can delegate. To achieve what is actually required of YOU in your job in one day a week or less, you need to ensure that you are the world's best delegator. Empower, engage, enthuse but make sure that above all else, people commit to a date to have things done and they meet that commitment with quality work every time. Make an art form out of delegation.

By the way, this strategy not only frees up your working week but gives you back your weekends. If you have become the model employee I suggest you do, through dedication and commitment, you probably spend at least half a day at the weekends "catching up". Instead, spend **half an hour** on Fridays ensuring that any reports others have promised that are not yet in will absolutely be on your desk by Monday. Then have the weekend off!

. the one day according to your work. If you are
. of job I was, you can spend half a day on
.g tasks, and then half a day on Friday

ensuring they have been completed. If your work has a diffent pattern, work within that. Maybe half an hour in the morning setting tasks and half an hour in the afternoon reviewing.

Great, six months after you read this, you've been promoted and you are the most efficient person in the company. Six months after that, you are working one day a week but still turning up to work of course! Now you have four days a week of uninterrupted time to do something really useful—learn how swing trade US stocks.

Once that's done you are ready to go to your boss and explain to him that you really are working only one day a week, that you are expensive and that there is a young person you know who you think could do the job perfectly well for much less salary.

There is no need to make this unpleasant. Despite what may be a burning desire to read your manager his fortune, keep everything amicable and pleasant. Partly this is because you don't want to burn bridges if there is no need, and partly to ensure that your departure is good from your perspective. No matter how well prepared you may be, there is an emotional element to leaving anyone or anything and you may as well be kind to yourself!

Depending on your organization, it may be better to go over your bosses head, to the Chairman, COO or HR. Just go to whomever it is who can actually make a fast decision—in many organizations that is one of only a very few people. Be well aware of the terms of your employment contract so that you can negotiate the best possible package. Keep focused on the cash components or things that can quickly be converted to cash. Naturally everyone will be happier if you explain that you are not going to a competitor, that you still love the company and that it is in the best interests of both you and the company for this to happen.

In today's climate redundancy is on the cards for absolutely everyone so my advice is to take full advantage of this to kickstart your new lifestyle.

Conclusion

I appreciate that I have written all this as if designing the lifestyle you wish to live and funding it were the simplest thing in the world. Maybe it's a tiny bit more complicated than I have made it but not much! I have aimed to de-mystify the stuff that people try to make complex.

The key is to understand "The Key" on page 150 and above all, to take responsibility for your life.

Most of this plan is not negotiable—if your goal is to leave work while you are still young enough to have an entire lifetime in front of you. That includes the trading part. It may be that you come across some other way of aking money that requires no staff and has no product, ting or distribution issues. Perhaps there is siness that requires only your knowledge and ked to the web to make fantastic profits.

If you ever do find such a business, jump on it! Its just that I have never run across anything as good as trading stocks.

You need that trading income because you do not want to live forever on the more or less fixed income stream from your properties. That's worse than working for someone else in my opinion. The property income is the security component of your financial freedom.

You want your income to increase every month, every year. You want cash to burn so that you can afford to change your lifestyle design when you choose. What about having a family—oops better quadruple that income requirement. Maybe your plan changes from hitchhiking around the planet to owning a super yacht in the Bahamas—might need a little bit more for that one! Property is the key to security, trading is the key to real money!

I have proven The Key works through trial and error. It has taken years of massive losses and taken its toll on relationships with family and friends. But those times have also taught me humility, and how to take responsibility for my own future.

Now you have the fundamentals to go and design a fantastic life and start working towards living it sooner rather than later. Start NOW.

ABOUT THE AUTHOR

Dennis Wall began the search for financial freedom at the age of 39. He "retired" ten years later. He strongly believes that anyone can do the same and that it's easier the younger you begin.

Today he lives roughly half his time in Singapore from where he manages his International property portfolio and trades US and Australian equities. The rest of his time is spent on his boat (named Playlife) which is moored in Phuket, Thailand.